George T. Wolz
March 29, 1971

*The Pearly Gates Syndicate, or
How to Sell Real Estate in Heaven*

The Pearly Gates Syndicate, or

CHARLES MERRILL SMITH

How to Sell Real Estate in Heaven

DOUBLEDAY & COMPANY, INC., GARDEN CITY, NEW YORK 1971

First Edition

This is for Dianne, Doug, and Terry

good kids

Contents

The Pearly Gates Syndicate, or
How to Sell Real Estate in Heaven

I. Introduction—Notes on a sorrowful condition and how to cure it

This is the story of the Pearly Gates Syndicate. It is a syndicate because it is a combine of agencies more or less united to merchandise a product. We call it the Pearly Gates Syndicate because the product it purveys is admission to heaven, real estate in paradise, assured entrance through the pearly gates. This product is often referred to as "salvation." The syndicate is commonly called "The Church."

You will find this story a treatise filled with hope, a source of good cheer in these admittedly gloomy days. Let us tell you why.

All patriotic, sound-thinking Americans are terribly worried over what appears, at first glance, to be our society coming apart at the seams. What upstanding American can view a protest march with equanimity? Who can look on the hippie culture without cringing? How are we to contemplate the untoward attacks on business and the military-industrial complex without resigning ourselves to an early end of the republic?

Furthermore, we are saddened by the present low estate of the Pearly Gates Syndicate. Some are even suggesting that what we are witnessing is the impending demise of the Church. Indeed, the decline of society in general, and the current weak state of health of the Church are not unrelated. This is why those who never go near a church—and there are millions of them—are concerned about the Pearly Gates Syndicate. They know, as well as those who show up every Sunday morning, that churches in the community undergird real estate values, bolster the Republican Party, encourage the kids to lay off sex and long hair, and fight harder than almost any other institution to curb socialistic tendencies and dangerous cultural experimentation which are such blatant threats to our way of life. "Who is going to do these things for us if the Church dies?" is a question on every lip.

We cannot conceal what, as of right now, are bleak and unpromising prospects for the Church. Tales of anguish emanate daily from the Vatican. Sunday school attendance is declining more rapidly than the Dow-Jones averages.[1] Cash receipts by parish churches and denominational or sectarian headquarters have plummeted to new lows. The church-building industry, which a few short years ago poured billions of dollars into our economy, is rumbling to a halt. Clergymen by the thousands are saying, "Oh, the hell with it," and forsaking their parishes for jobs in the poverty program or the selling of life insurance. Nobody much goes to church any more except in those sections of the country commonly referred to as the Bible belt, which have staunchly resisted the corrosions of the modern world. In most of the nation's major cities there are large and prestigious churches where, a few years ago, you had to push and shove for a seat at Sunday worship. Today these churches are all but depopulated at 11 A.M. on the Lord's day.

ANTIDOTE FOR DISCOURAGEMENT

Are we then to despair? Must we passively await the hearse of history to cart away the remains of the religious institution? Has an irreversible *rigor mortis* already set in?

Of course not. If we only had a proper perspective, we would realize that what the Church is now suffering is not a terminal distemper but only a temporary touch of indigestion. But even indigestion must be treated lest, long neglected, it prove fatal.

This book is written to help correct the sorrowful condition

[1] Kids never did go to Sunday school because they wanted to go, as we all know. They went because their parents made them go. We look with alarm on this increasing disinclination of parents to force their kids to attend Sunday school, and view it as one of the surer signs of national decay.

described above. Though scholarly in content, it is popular in style, directed to those millions of churchmen, either intensely religious, mildly loyal, or nominal, as well as to the religiously indifferent and the atheistic who believe that religion is good for other people and is necessary to the stability of our society.

SEEKING THE RIGHT IMAGE

It is our thesis, furthermore, that all the Church's troubles stem from faulty and inexact concepts of what the Church is. It fails to present to the public a proper company image.

Let us illustrate. Thumb through any hymnal and notice the most frequently recurring metaphors for the Church. By all odds the most popular is some variation on the picture of the Church as "like a mighty army." We turn up, also, several comparisons of the Church to a kingdom, a rock, a city of righteousness, and even esoterica such as "Cool Siloam's shady rill." While all these examples are lovely poetic images, and we have not a word of criticism to hurl against them, they are not up to doing the job for us today.

We are proposing, therefore, a new metaphor for the Church. It must be a concept modern in design, vigorous in nature, practical in operation, evocative of admiration, symbolic of the best in our twentieth-century society.

The military metaphor, of course, fulfills these conditions. We considered it because, as reflected by the size of its appropriation in the national budget, it has a hold on the affections of the people seldom surpassed by any institution.[2] But we discarded it because, first, it has been used for so long as a mind picture of the Church that it has lost its freshness. Second, we discarded it because we have a livelier alternative. We believe there is no better way to think of the Church than as a modern business corporation.

[2] We are aware that the Pentagon is not universally admired, but are pretty certain that its critics are mostly agnostics, vegetarians, and other reprehensible types. You hardly ever hear any criticism of the Pentagon from churchgoers.

THE CHRISTIAN CORPORATION

It is possible, we know, that some people will be offended by likening the Church to a business corporation. But surely it is no worse than the commonly accepted poetic images of the Church. Comparing the Church to a city, which so many of our best-loved hymns do, leaves something to be desired, considering the prevailing conditions in our modern cities. Kingdoms were splendid to behold at one time, but kingdoms aren't what they used to be.[3] A rock is a sturdy image, to be sure, but somewhat lacking in viability. And we cannot see, for the life of us, why anyone who is not offended by singing "like a mighty army" would be offended by singing "like a corporation." It would be no problem at all, we are convinced, to persuade the average congregation to think affectionately of the Church as a business corporation if only it had some hymns to sing which projected the corporate image with verve and style. These can be written, of course, and we are confident they will be written. To show you the kind of hymns we need we have written one ourself. It is to be sung to the tune of "Onward, Christian Soldiers." It is entitled "Christian Corporation." It goes like this:

> Christian Corporation, marching to the bank
> Doing Christian business, hear the money clank;
> Success our ruling passion, power our greatest prize,
> In the name of Jesus, who can criticize?

refrain

> Christian Corporation, moving to the top
> Holy Aspirations! nothing us can stop

> Like a Corporation,
> moves the Church once more
> execs, we are likened, to those men of yore
> Popes and bishops royal, splendid clergy too
> Who led the Corporation, then, as now we do.

refrain

[3] We were all depressed to hear that things are so bad in The United Kingdom that Prince Philip can no longer afford to maintain his stable of polo ponies.

Now that we have put to rest any queasiness you may have felt at our first mention of the business corporation as the new metaphor for the Church, we will get on with illustrating its advantages. From this point on we shall refer to the Church as the Christian Corporation or the Pearly Gates Syndicate. The terms are interchangeable.

We aim to tell you the story of the Church, from the beginning down till now. While you could read the story in any one of thousands of church histories available, none of them tell it in terms of the Church as a corporation. We shall demonstrate through our re-telling of the story that the Church, for seventeen hundred years, approximately, of its existence has in fact behaved—on and off—very much like a modern business corporation. Furthermore, we shall see that it was at its glorious best in those times when it acted in accordance with modern business practice, and well-nigh disabled when forsaking these sound principles.

We shall tell you the story for another reason. It is our theory, hardly disputable, that the dejection we feel about the low estate of the Church today will not disappear until the people know more about its history than they now know, which is very little.[4] Being unsullied by any information on the Church's past, they are unable to evaluate objectively its precarious present. They think its current state of the blahs marks the nadir of the Christian Corporation, whereas, in fact, things have often been much worse. And with minds unencumbered by knowledge of the Corporation's former glories, they are unable to envision a triumphant future. But things are bound to get better. They always have.

---

[4] To discover the present level of the average man's knowledge of church history, the author commissioned a scientific survey to be made among a carefully selected cross section of the American churchgoing public. Among the information uncovered was that 78.3 per cent of those Christians responding thought that the Epistles were the wives of the Apostles; 81.9 per cent identified the Semi-Pelagians as a new rock-and-roll performing group; and an astonishing 88.6 per cent were convinced that Antinomianism is a disease of the circulatory system.

WHY THE FIRST THREE HUNDRED YEARS ARE UNIMPORTANT

Like all scholars we have had to be selective in what we tell you. There is ample material to fill forty or fifty volumes, but you do not need to know that much about church history. We have restricted ourselves, therefore, to the salient points.

Furthermore, we shall tell the story pretty much in terms of the personalities who created it—saints, martyrs, soldiers brave and pious, popes, bishops, kings, reformers, preachers, people like this. We will find some of them more appealing than others, of course. When we are inclined to be censorious of one or more of these Christian heroes, we must remember that each and every one was serving the Christian Corporation as he saw fit in order to earn his salvation. Such a noble motivation makes everything they did perfectly acceptable to God, and if God accepts it we have to accept it.

All scholars also have a point of view from which they write their histories. We have already said that our perspective is that of the Church as a business corporation. Therefore, we won't linger long on the first three hundred years of church history because those are its precorporation days. During this period it was small, fragmented, unrelated to the society and politics of its time. It was frequently in trouble with the state and the power structure because it would not conform to the proven, accepted values and mores of the day. In short, it had not yet learned how to act as a corporation.[5]

After the Emperor Constantine made of it a legal corporation—a story we shall be telling you shortly—the Church mastered the most important lesson life has to teach us, which is that it is always better for you if you get along with city hall. Or to put it another way, after Constantine, the Church altered its stance from anti-establishment to pro-establishment. It began acting like a true corporation.

[5] It didn't even have a public relations department as yet.

THE ADVANTAGES OF JOINING THE ESTABLISHMENT

This improvement in the Church's attitude, of course, paid off handsomely. Whereas it had been persecuted, it was now accepted. Before Constantine, church members were forever being burned at the stake or chewed up by lions in the arena. After Constantine, joining the Church was the chic thing to do and, except for brief periods, entailed no discomfort or danger whatever.[6]

To simplify our perspective even further, when we judge the performance of a pope or saint or Christian king or any churchman who has played a significant role in Christian history, we have asked ourselves the question, "Did he react as Richard Nixon would have reacted under similar circumstances?" If the answer is Yes, then we rate the performance very highly. And when we evaluate the activities of the Church as a corporation, we pose this query: "Is this how General Motors would have handled it?" Again, if the answer is Yes, we shall have no fault to find whatsoever. We can imagine no surer standards, no truer tests by which to measure the heroes of the faith and the Christian Corporation.

[6] After Constantine, the non-Christians frequently suffered persecution by the Christians, which seems only fair.

II. *The pre-corporation days—the first three centuries*

From our modern, enlightened understanding of how the Church at its best should perform, as we have just described it, we know that all the real progress came after the first three hundred years. But careful scholarship requires us to include a brief account of those early years because a few fairly significant events did occur in that period. Also, it is necessary that you know at least a sketchy outline of the first three centuries in order that you may understand what is going on when we get to the important stuff. If you don't know what it was like in the early, crude days, you will be unable to appreciate the vast and rapid progress of the Christian Corporation.

The logical place to begin would be with Jesus, but to repeat that story would be superfluous as everyone knows it frontward and backward already. There was a time when the Church emphasized the less-attractive aspects of Jesus' life, such as his refusal to accept the authority of the religious establishment, and his unwillingness to observe the laws of the Sabbath, the ritual washings, and other folkways and mores of his society. Some people have even had the temerity to suggest that he was essentially a radical and a rebel. Such a picture of Jesus, had it prevailed, would have been a disaster for the Christian Corporation.[1] It didn't take long to dis-

[1] Some of Jesus' teachings have also caused occasional distress to the Christian Corporation. "The meek shall inherit the earth," for example, not only is incompatible with all theories of successful corporation management, but strikes the modern mind as sheer nonsense.

cover, though, that Jesus can be presented as the original positive thinker, master of selling techniques, or an unbendable advocate of whatever your national aspirations and cultural values of the moment may be.[2]

THE INADEQUACIES OF THE APOSTLES

The apostles, too, present us with something of a problem. We hasten to make it clear that our admiration for the disciples, excepting one, of course, is unbounded. After all, they were the first church, the original Christian Corporation. They came, however, from a level of society lower than that from which successful corporations normally draw their leadership. Also, they simply didn't understand the arts of business organization, public relations, promoting the product, advertising, etc.—the very arts, in fact, which are so basic to the success of any corporation. It is only right that we should honor and revere the disciples and even make saints out of them, but it would be fatal to the corporation if we made the mistake of imitating their methods. If you want your enterprise to succeed—and all right-thinking people do want their enterprises to succeed—then you must find successful men to lead it. The disciples, however good, were losers.

So we shall skip over the part about Jesus and the disciples, not only because of the reasons stated but also because it doesn't figure too prominently in the story anyway.

HOW THE CORPORATION WAS NAMED

Let us begin, then, with the naming of our Christian Corporation, although this happened long before it was a corporation in any true sense of the word.

The Corporation, as you know, named itself "church." The original

[2] It is a favorite device of restricted residential developments and country clubs to admit white Christians only. Jesus, who as a Middle-Eastern peasant was not too white and was a Jew, would be excluded from the development or the club in his own name, but nobody is so stupid as to bring this up.

Greek word for church was *ecclesia* which means "those who are called." It is a very nice word and appealed strongly to Greeks and mystics and intellectuals. But before long it was felt that the term was a bit too vague for practical, down-to-earth people. So another name, with more sales appeal was sought. The Corporation settled on the word *Kyriakon,* also Greek, which means "the Lord's house."

Now that is more like it. A house is not a misty abstraction like "those who are called." It has to be built and managed and financed. It is tangible. It is, furthermore, a fine symbol for a business, which is what a corporation is. The final choice of a name was the first sound business decision the Church made. We shall assume, then, that *Kyriakon* is the original word from which the name and the idea "church" is derived, which is only fudging a little on historical accuracy.

In its very early days the Church didn't have much that can be described as an organization, but it did have some. At that time all Christians expected that the world would come to an end any day.[3] So it didn't seem important to them to build fancy church buildings and put together a first-rate scheme of organization.

But they discovered that some organization was necessary. Even though all Christians at that time loved one another, which, regrettably, they don't today, there was a considerable amount of Christian fussing and feuding. They quarreled over who would get the best seats at the Lord's Supper[4] and similar significant issues, so it became apparent that there would have to be a headman to settle these Christian controversies. So the custom of electing an *episkopos* for each congregation got started. *Episkopos* is a Greek word which, roughly translated, means "a guy who keeps an eye on pious shenanigans in the Church." As time went on the word got corrupted to "bishop," although, of course, the office wasn't cor-

[3] That the world will come to an end any day now is a belief which seems as sensible to us as it did to the early Christians, although for not exactly the same reasons.

[4] Today it is the back seats which are in largest demand at church services. But in those early days the Lord's Supper was not a thimbleful of Welch's Grape Juice and a bite of bread. It was a full meal, more like our modern church potluck dinner than anything else we can think of. So it was important to be up front where the grub was, or some Christians who hadn't been completely saved from the sin of gluttony would hog everything.

rupted but went on to new levels of power and glory, culminating —as we shall see presently—in the office of pope, who is like chairman of the board. Actually, the pope does exactly what the first *episkopos* did, but of course at a higher level.

THE BEGINNINGS OF THE HIERARCHY—A PROMISE OF FUTURE MAGNIFICENCE

We must not fail to stress the magnitude of the decision to elect a congregational chief to tell people where to sit in church. From this humble beginning came the magnificence of the episcopal office. More important still, it was the first step in the creation of a hierarchy. Hierarchy means "the rule of the high priest," but the true significance of a hierarchy is that when you have one you have a corporation.

Once the Church had decided on having bishops it was able to see that you need to invest the bishop with certain trappings of office in order to lend dignity and weight to his decisions. People will accept a decision even if they don't like it very well so long as the decider is, in their mind, someone of importance. The way you make someone important is to pretend that he is important, or rather that the position he occupies is important.

The early Church was made up of poor people, quite different from the Church today we are glad to say, so they couldn't build a gorgeous building to house the bishop. They didn't even have the price of splendid habiliments for their *episkopos*. But they were ingenious. It was stipulated that when rendering his decisions the bishop would sit in a special chair reserved only for him. They did have the price of a chair. When the time came for the Church to have buildings of its own, the chair was placed in a church build-ing. Since the word for chair was *cathedra,* a church building with a bishop's chair in it came to be called a cathedral.[5] Today a

---

[5] You have, we expect, always thought that cathedral meant a great big church building, preferably Gothic. This is because the Christian Corporation learned long ago that great big church buildings, preferably Gothic, are most dazzling to the lay mind and thus better for the institutional image than little bitty church buildings, as well as more consistent with the dignity of a bishop. But a little bitty church building can be a cathedral if it has a bishop's chair in it, and there are some such cathedrals, although not many.

desk—usually massive and costly—is a more fitting symbol for the office of bishop than a chair, but the chair is retained for sentimental reasons.

THE ODD BEHAVIOR OF THE EARLY CHRISTIANS

All literate people associate the pre-corporation, or before-Constantine days of the Church, with persecution of Christians by torture, burning, imprisonment and a variety of distasteful devices thought up by the Roman authorities. You are perhaps wondering why anyone would want to persecute the early Christians as we have described them up to now. Problems arose soon, though, because these early Christians simply could not grasp the importance of getting along with the politicians and accommodating their attitudes to the beliefs and practices of society.

For example, they offended people by refusing to go to the hospital when they were sick. This was not because they were Christian Scientists. Christian Science hadn't been invented yet. It was because back then hospital chaplains were pagan priests. Today, if pagans refused to go to a hospital because hospital chaplains are Christian priests we would rightly be indignant, so we can understand why the early Christians incurred the hostility of their society.

Then, in those days, many Christians earned their living as stonecutters. Stonecutters, then as now, do most of their business in the tombstone line. But these Christians wouldn't carve any pagan gods on tombstones even though a customer was a pagan and wanted pagan gods carved for him, which most of them did. The Christian stonecutter would say, "No, I can't carve a pagan god for you, but I do very nice lion's heads or whales. How about a nice lion's head or whale?" Lion's heads and whales were not big sellers, however, and this caused a lot of needless unemployment among Christian stonecutters because they hadn't learned then what we modern Christians know, which is that the customer is always right.

We wouldn't view the refusal to carve pagan gods on tombstones as terribly offensive, but it is difficult for us to understand the Christians' disinclination to attend the gladiatorial combats in the

arena. Such an attitude is comparable to a modern Christian refusing
to attend a professional football game or at least watch it on
television. Professional football is much like gladiatorial combat,
what with its helmets and breastplates and violent attempts to maim
or kill one's opponent, and we have yet to hear a modern Christian
object to the good clean fun of professional football. It would be
almost unpatriotic to do so. The Romans felt that folks who are
censorious of society's favorite pastimes are potential threats to national security, a conviction that is difficult to refute.

We do not wish to give the impression that the early Christians
were totally unco-operative with the duly constituted authorities.
They were docile enough in the matter of keeping slaves. In those
days it was not only legal but customary for wealthy people to own
slaves. Wealthy Christians, of which there were a few back then
though of course not so many as now, kept slaves because, not
only would it have upset society if they hadn't, but also who would
have done their menial work for them? A fact which emerges from
the study of history is that wealthy people, Christian or otherwise,
always see more clearly the importance of co-operating with society
than poor people do. Anyway, Christians were supposed to treat
their slaves kindly, and we have no reason to believe that they
didn't.

But the early Christians wouldn't go to war, and no one can
blame the Roman government, which had gotten where it was by
going to war, for looking on this as subversive.

Also, the early Christians held the service of the Lord's Supper
in secret. This caused no little talk among the neighbors, not all of
it good. Some people said the Christians were meeting in secret
because they were plotting against the government. Others, who had
probably heard snatches of the liturgy the Christians employed at
Holy Communion, spread the story that Christians were cannibals,
a false but not unreasonable conclusion.

After all, critics have been claiming for years that Christians
eat their God. While we think this surly and pejorative of the
critics, we admit that, on the basis of a literal reading of the Mass
or Eucharist or Communion service, the charge has a certain cogency.

Since politicians, then as now, are rather paranoid in their reaction to any group meeting in secret, and because civilized people usually look on cannibalism as unacceptable, practically everybody said something had to be done about the Christians—and that's how the persecutions got started.

We have a picture of the hard-eyed Roman Gestapo relentlessly pursuing the early Christians, sort of like a grade-B Nazi movie with the gauleiters hunting down Hebrews, but it wasn't like that at all, or at least not at first. Actually, many of the officials who had the job of persecuting Christians didn't really want to and would often try to talk the Christians into making a *pro forma*[6] recantation so that they wouldn't have to burn them or throw them to the lions.

POLYCARP'S ANTI-INCENSE POSITION

One famous early Christian martyr was an aged bishop named Polycarp. The high sheriff, whose job it was to execute Christians but who didn't like it much, said to him, "Polycarp, this is silly. It escapes me why you refuse to say 'Caesar is Lord' and sprinkle a little incense on the pagan altar, especially as sprinkling incense around is a very nice custom and I'll bet you Christians will be doing it yourselves one of these days." But Polycarp said No, so they dragged him into the arena where there was a sellout crowd. The governor was acting as master of ceremonies, and he didn't want to persecute Polycarp either. He offered to let the old boy off if he would make a speech about Christianity and persuade the crowd that it was O.K. to be a Christian. But Polycarp said he wouldn't, which we find hard to understand because Billy Graham and Oral Roberts have to go to all kinds of trouble and expense today to draw crowds like that to preach to, and this one wasn't costing Polycarp a cent. Anyway, they finally had to execute Polycarp. Some say it was by burning, and others say he was stabbed, and there are those who claim they let the lions eat him, but it really doesn't make much difference.

[6] A *pro forma* recantation was just for the record, as these officials didn't mind if Christians went on being Christians as long as they said they weren't.

During the first three hundred years there was an enormous amount of persecution of Christians. However, it didn't happen every day, and there were long periods when the government was either tired of it or bored with it and didn't persecute Christians at all. We have the idea, inculcated by sentimental and ill-informed Sunday-school teachers, whose severest Christian suffering consisted of getting rained on en route to church, that persecution and martyrdom are healthy for the faith, but they aren't. During the periods of persecution, the early church would go underground and lose a lot of members, because you have to want to be a Christian pretty badly when you know that to be one might get you the hot seat.

On the other hand, when the government laid off the persecution for prolonged periods, the Church would become rather popular and enjoy rapid growth in members, and Sunday collections would go way up. From about A.D. 200 to 250 there was hardly any persecution and everyone relaxed and said, "It looks like we've got it made."

THE PIOUS PAGANISM OF THE EMPEROR DECIUS

But they hadn't. About A.D. 250 the Emperor Decius, known as Decius the Pious because he was a pious and devout pagan,[7] decided the time had come to rid the empire of Christians. He said he had to clean out the Christians because Christians were atheists. We may be surprised at this until we remember that an atheist is simply a fellow who doesn't believe in and worship the popular, accepted god or gods exalted by current culture. If Decius came back to life and tried to run for the Senate, we would accuse him of being an atheist because he didn't believe that Yahweh is a white Anglo-Saxon who likes America best, and only Madelyn Murray O'Hair and a few other strange types would vote for him. We wouldn't throw him to the lions of course, so this marks some progress, although many Christians would want to do pretty bad things to him.

[7] It may come as a shock to many Christians to learn that a pagan could be called pious because Christians have usually assumed that Christians have an exclusive franchise on piety.

Decius also said that Christians were pests and a threat to established authority, not too different from our attitude toward Father Groppi and Chaplain William Sloane Coffin, so we can be somewhat sympathetic toward Decius and his problem. Decius drew up a form which said that you affirm you are a good, loyal, pious pagan and that you sacrificed to the gods regularly and all that. He announced that everyone had to sign it, a demand no more unreasonable than the loyalty oaths we force public employees to take today, and hardly anybody but commies and subversives object to them.

Decius' decree could have gone a long way toward wiping out the young church, as he was in no mood to fool around with recalcitrants. By this time, though, the Church had learned a thing or two about getting along with the world. Although there are always some bullheaded Christians around who won't knuckle under to reasonable public and social pressure, a lot of Christians were pretty tired of the persecution scene and figured out how to get around it.

If you want to enforce a thorough loyalty program you have to set up a vast bureaucracy to administer it, which is what Decius did. A few smart Christians who understood the doctrine of original sin suspected that the bureaucrats were underpaid and quite susceptible to bribes. So the popular Christian strategy was to bribe the officials to give you a certificate saying you were a good pious pagan, but the official wouldn't make you sacrifice. That way, a Christian could keep a good clear Christian conscience about sacrificing to the gods and also avoid the discomfort of being persecuted.

Another Christian strategy was for the bishop to round up his whole congregation and say to them, "Friends, let's go to the nearest pagan temple and sprinkle some incense around and get our certificates because sacrificing to the gods doesn't mean anything really, it's just like getting a license for your chariot or a receipt for your income tax." Then the congregation would do this. But it created a lot of hostility in the public official who had to give them their certificates because it cheated him out of his rightful bribe money, although there wasn't anything he could do about it.

However, the Decian persecution didn't last very long because it was a costly program to administer, and some economy advocates in the senate, who weren't as pious as Decius, said they should be spending public money on something more beneficial to the economy, such as the military-industrial complex maybe, so that was the end of that.[8]

Now the Church had a problem. The Christians who hadn't sacrificed to the pagan gods and had been put in the pokey for their intransigent attitude thought they were the only true Christians left. So what was the Church to do? If it sided with the Christians who had bribed or sacrificed, it would be giving tacit approval to Christian lying and cheating, which isn't a good idea. On the other hand, if it sided with the Christians who hadn't bribed or cheated and kicked all the others out, it would have decreased the Church's membership rolls by the hundreds of thousands, an even worse idea.

HOW TO PUNISH SINNERS WITHOUT LOSING CUSTOMERS

The Church's solution to the problem was something we never would have thought of. It sat down and wrote some theology, or perhaps more accurately some biblical exegesis.[9] It was discovered by exegesis that a bishop had the power to forgive sins on earth and then they would automatically be forgiven in heaven, and this is what they wrote down and made into doctrine.

Nobody argued against this exegetical discovery, at least not much. So the Church said all Christians who had sacrificed to the gods or bribed Roman officials to say they had would be welcomed back into the fold of the faithful, and the bishop would forgive their sins just as soon as they proved they were sorry. To prove that you were sorry you had to do two things. You had to appear before the congregation and confess your sins. And you had to put on sackcloth clothes, which aren't very stylish and besides they make you

[8] This is a case of piety yielding to economics. In nearly every such case piety yields to economics.

[9] For the handful of our readers who may be unfamiliar with the term, exegesis is the science or art of explaining what the writers of the Bible meant by what they said. Exegesis is particularly helpful when you need the Bible to back you up. A highly skilled exegete can frequently extract two diametrically opposed meanings from the same passage of Scripture.

itch, and put ashes on your head to show your contrition even though this messed up the ladies' hairdos.

Resorting to exegesis, about as impractical an activity as you can think of, turned out to be one of the most practical, hard-headed ploys the Church ever conceived, although it probably didn't know it when it was doing it. By exegesis the Church took two giant steps toward becoming a genuine corporation.

First, by letting a bishop forgive sins, it greatly enhanced the power and prestige of that office. As any businessman will tell you, you can't have a corporation that amounts to anything until people know who is boss. Now everybody knew that the bishop was boss.

Second, the Church quickly caught on to the fact that "penance" and "confession" had a far greater potential than just letting a few sinners sneak back into the fold. Although the concept of man as conceived in sin and born in corruption had not as yet been formally articulated as the doctrine of original sin, nonetheless the early church fathers had some inkling that not everyone is going to live a perfect Christian life even though they have been soundly converted. They perceived that, rather than temporary expedients, penance and confession could be employed as permanent techniques for the merchandising of salvation. The idea that the Church could at any time provide you with forgiveness for your sins through penance and confession was, as we shall see later, the foundation stone in the Church's corporate success.

As time went on, the Church had to modify how you did your penance and confession, though. People objected to wearing itchy sackcloth and messing up their hair with ashes, so the Church substituted things like saying extra Hail Marys and paternosters for penance, and this was found more acceptable. For a while, all confessions were made in front of the congregation. However, sometimes these confessions got pretty racy and people liked to hear them better than the sermon, so the Church decided it was best for confessions to be made privately to a priest.

There was one more big push on persecutions before the Church teamed up with the empire and put a stop to this nonsense.[10] This

---

[10] Put a stop to the nonsense of pagans persecuting Christians, that is. The Church has never considered that Christians persecuting pagans, or for that

was under the Emperor Diocletian, who tore down churches and tore up Bibles and did other boorish and nasty things. Diocletian especially liked to bag the clergy, and a lot of them knuckled under when the heat was on, and then wanted back in when it was off.

As we know, the Church had already decided that mere laymen could be forgiven for tossing in the sponge in the face of persecution. However, just as is the case today, the clergy was supposed to be a different order of being, what we might call "superchristians." The clergy isn't vulnerable, according to the image in the lay mind, to the temptations which make it so difficult for laymen to get to heaven. When some of the clergy behaved no better than the laity it was a profound shock to many. It was argued that the amnesty extended to the laity should not be offered to the clergy. The Church wisely decided, though, that you have to forgive the clergy too because if you don't you can lose an awful lot of clergymen.

This time not everyone agreed. Some Christians who were pretty sore about it went off to pout and found a new Christian church. The new sect, which called themselves "Donatists," wouldn't admit anyone to membership who had sacrificed to the gods or bribed Roman officials.

The Donatists, who for some reason attracted huge numbers of the poor and discontented and the lower classes in general, exhibited what we would consider an uncharitable spirit toward their brethren of the one true church. The Donatists liked to tear down non-Donatist church buildings, which seems like a dirty trick to us. Their favorite dirty trick was to sneak into the service of a regular or true Christian church pretending to be regular or true Christian worshipers. Then, when the bishop wasn't looking, they would throw acid in his eyes. This didn't improve relations very much between the two Christian groups. Finally, the orthodox or true Christians had to get a law passed that the penalty for being a Donatist was death.

---

matter Christians persecuting Christians who wouldn't stay in line, is nonsense. It has more or less indulged in this sort of thing ever since it has had enough muscle to get away with it.

People today sometimes censure such measures as overly severe, but it takes severe measures to discourage Donatists. The Church, even in its infancy, had already grasped the principle of stifling the competition. It learned early that when you can brand the competition "heresy," nearly everyone is enthusiastic about stamping it out. This strategy has paid off handsomely for the Church throughout its entire history.

III. *Constantine takes over as emperor—* *the Christians' big break*

Diocletian was worn out after persecuting all those Christians, so he retired from being emperor.

Back then, when the emperorship fell vacant, it was not too different from when our presidency falls vacant. Many aspirants for the job put themselves forward as being best qualified. Today candidates do battle on TV, and the one who can buy the most TV prime time plus of course the best of make-up men and stage directors wins the presidency. In the fourth century the custom was for the candidates for emperor to fight it out with their personal armies, and the candidate who could pay for the biggest army usually was acclaimed emperor.

For a successor to Diocletian the decision finally boiled down to a choice between two assistant emperors. One was named Maxentius and the other one's name was Constantine. Both of them had pretty good armies so the contest was rated at even money, or maybe six to five and take your pick. The evening before the battle was similar to the eve of the Notre Dame-Southern Cal game. Each side was trying to get itself psyched up for the slaying on the morrow.

Constantine went out to look at the sunset and think moody thoughts such as this might be the last sunset he would ever see. Suddenly there appeared in the sky above the sun a cross made out of light, and also—in bold, upper-case Roman type face—the words IN HOC SIGNO VINCES. As you know, this means "By this sign conquer."[1] Constantine, of course, was impressed, as it isn't every day you see this sort of thing. He had been around enough to know that a cross was the symbol of the Christian God. He reasoned that if the Christian God was able to slap big signs above the sun written in grammatical Latin, he must be a god with plenty of clout, so maybe it would be a good idea to serve him— for tomorrow's battle at least. And indeed, dedicating the battle to the Christian God was the soundest political decision Constantine could have made, as well as the biggest break that ever came the way of the Church. First, he won the battle without even working up a sweat. He just backed Maxentius and his troops into the Tiber River where a lot of them drowned, including Maxentius.[2]

Second, from this experience Constantine gathered that the Christian God was a pretty good god to serve inasmuch as he could evidently deliver the goods, so he abolished the persecution of Christians and made Christianity the most favored religion of the empire. The Church then began co-operating with society and the government, and after this there was no holding it, even if it did have troubles from time to time, as we shall see.

Let us now examine how Constantine transformed a proscribed sect into the dominant religious organization of the Roman Empire.

How heartwarming it would be to report that Constantine was thoroughly converted to Christianity and became a fervent follower of the Church. Our pious desire is to tell you this because it would make for a more inspiring story. But as a conscientious historian, we have to say that there is no solid evidence that Constantine himself ever embraced the faith.

---

[1] Some authorities claim it only read *Hoc Signo Vinces,* but the general drift of the message is the same.

[2] What actually happened was that Maxentius' troops were in such a hurry to get the hell out of there that too many of them crowded onto a bridge and it broke, dumping Maxentius and practically his whole army into the drink. Since the bridge that busted was named the Milvian Bridge, this battle is known in history as the battle of the Milvian Bridge—although it wasn't much of a battle, and it wasn't much of a bridge.

THE ADVANTAGES AND DISADVANTAGES OF DEATHBED BAPTISM

You have probably heard the story that Constantine was baptized on his deathbed. Modern Christians are sometimes cynical about deathbed repentance and think it only slightly better than shuffling off this mortal coil unshriven. We need to understand that in the early days of the Church deathbed baptism was in good odor, and in some areas the recommended practice.[3] The theory was that, since baptism washes away sin but you can only be baptized once, it is better to save it until you have lost your taste for sinning. Many people have a taste for sinning until quite late in life. Some extremely robust persons, such as Constantine, don't lose it until they are almost pegged out or completely immobilized. So we can see the logic of the practice.

Deathbed baptism did have disadvantages. A priest might be finishing his dessert when you sent for him and he wouldn't get there before you gave up the ghost, and then you would be in a pickle. On the other hand, you might mistake a severe but curable cases of influenza for a terminal flux and hastily submit to sprinkling. Upon recovery you would face many years of healthy sinning in the baptized state without the possibility of a second dousing. That would leave you in a worse pickle. You can see that in the practice of deathbed baptism timing is most important.

But we aren't certain that Constantine was baptized at all. What we are certain of is that he saw the political possibilities in a strong Christian church. He knew that a healthy, prosperous religious establishment, which can be counted on to bless and give God's approval to whatever the state was up to at the moment, is absolutely essential to the efficient and trouble-free operation of a government. In our time President Eisenhower expressed much the

[3] St. Augustine wanted to be baptized at an early age, but his saintly mother discouraged him on the grounds that it was unrealistic to suppose he had done all his sinning. As it turned out, he hadn't. But after a lengthy sojourn in the tents of wickedness he did get baptized and became a bishop. Since this enabled him to have the best of both worlds, we expect he was awfully grateful for the good parental advice he had received.

same sentiment when he counseled us not to worry about what we believed in, just believe. Politicians are always more partial to the practical application of religion to life than they are to piety, even though you come across a politician now and then who is personally as pious as anyone could want.

Anyway, Constantine didn't care particularly what religion the people of the Roman Empire had so long as everybody, or almost everybody, had the same one. Whether he picked Christianity because it was the most popular, or the best organized religion, or because the Christian God had helped him paste Maxentius, or for a combination of these reasons, he picked it.

Christianity wasn't exactly made the state religion under Constantine, though many uninformed people think that it was. Constantine, a superb psychologist, knew that for a religion to have any potency people need to feel, or at least pretend, that they joined it of their own free will and for what they tell themselves are spiritual reasons. He suspected that people, the masses anyway, join a religion for reasons having nothing whatever to do with spirituality —such as because it is popular, or socially advantageous, or is a source of promising business contacts, or is good politics, or for any number of other laudable but not exactly spiritual reasons.[4]

What Constantine did, at first, was to make little changes which upgraded the status of the Church.

For example, he put the monogram of Christ on the coins of the realm, although he didn't take off the old pagan symbol, which may well have made them the first ecumenical coins. The pagan symbol which stayed on the coins was a wolf, and when people would object to a bishop that these coins were half-pagan, which they sometimes did, the bishop would reply, "the wolf is now a Christian wolf." Pagan or Christian, the coins were good, hard, spendable currency, so Christian objection to them soon disappeared and the Church found them perfectly acceptable in payment of your weekly pledge to the budget.

---

[4] That people join a religion for other than purely spiritual reasons has not been lost on present-day pastors. Read the church ads in any Saturday paper encouraging you to "worship with us in air-conditioned comfort" or "say your prayers while kneeling on our padded, tapestry-covered prayer pillows" and you will see that Constantine has had a beneficent influence on the Church that has not abated with the years.

Next, Constantine put a Christian monogram on the battle standards of his regiments. Our first reaction here is that the symbol of a pacifist religion is hardly the ideal monogram for an army, and we would have expected the Christians to veto the plan. But after thinking it over, the Church adopted the view that since it was beyond argument that Jehovah had sent Constantine to deliver Christians from persecution, Constantine was God's man and his wars were godly wars. Looked at in such a light anyone could see that Constantine's military activity didn't clash in any way with the Church's pacifist convictions.

We have here a geniune step forward in the Church's understanding of its relationship to the state. This line of reasoning has made it possible for the Christian Corporation to be first, last and always unalterably opposed to war in general, but at the same time to support any particular war which comes along on the grounds that it is God's will for us to win this one.

CONSTANTINE CULTIVATES THE CLERGY

Another particle in the mosaic of politico-religious co-operation Constantine was putting together was the enlistment of the Christian clergy in his cause. In 319 he passed a law which said that the clergy was excused from "public obligations," meaning that preachers didn't have to pay taxes or serve in the army. Gifts of cash were bestowed upon the clergy personally as well as the Church. Christian bishops were allowed to ride in government coaches free of charge, and providing travel expenses in a wonderful way to make the free riders like you and use their influence for whatever you want done, as our senators and congressmen are demonstrating practically every day.

The emperor also rebuilt the churches destroyed by his predecessors and punished the pagans for their depredations by sending them the bill, a painful retribution indeed. Then he built some new churches out of his own pocket, including St. Sophia at Constantinople, one of early Christianity's showcases, now unfortunately fallen into the hands of the infidel and turned into a Mohammedan mosque.

Other kings and emperors have been awfully nice to the Church, of course, showering it with cash and favors. Constantine, however, is responsible for the unique blessing, the one great favor, the most princely of princely gifts to the Church. It was Constantine who transformed it from a promising but inadequate business into a true corporation worthy of being listed on the big board. In the year 321 he granted the Church the right to receive legacies and bequests, and, as one eminent historian puts it, "thereby the privileges of the church *as a corporation*[5] (were) acknowledged."

THE BLESSINGS OF CORPORATE STATUS

Try to envision what Constantine's simple act has accomplished for the Church. Over the last seventeen hundred years it has amassed mind-boggling amounts of real estate, cash, gold, gems, gilt-edged securities, buildings, businesses, etc.—and every nickel of it beyond the clutch of the tax collector! All well-disposed people now recognize that, since the Church is spiritual in nature and therefore not tempted to the sins of pride and avarice which beset very rich secular corporations, it shouldn't be taxed. It's only right. But to Constantine belongs the honor and glory of having recognized it first.[6]

We regret to report that the tax-free status enjoyed by the Church is at present under attack from some misguided and unspiritual legislators on the lookout for new sources of tax revenue, and since they have squeezed dry almost everything else, they are turning their greedy gaze on the church and its vast wealth.

We must fight them valorously. Think of the dire consequences to our way of life if the Church is taxed. For example, most cities and towns and villages are saturated with churches, each with a resident pastor or pastors attached. If the Church had to pay taxes, it

---

[5] The italics are ours, as this historian evidently didn't grasp the true significance of these three words.

[6] It is possible, of course, that some bishop or ecclesiastical official helped him to recognize it.

couldn't support all these buildings and clergy. It would have to consolidate and merge, causing unemployment among the clergy and loss of income to the public utilities. It would eliminate denominational competition, reduce drastically the strength of the army of the Lord, shrink our sectarian options, kill off the church building industry, to mention only a few of the terrible side effects. There would be a chain reaction which would eventually mean fewer bishops and denominational executives, and since bishops and denominational executives have large office establishments, a flourishing employment market for secretaries and stenographers and receptionists would be curtailed. Manufacturers of mimeograph machines and typewriters and all classes of office equipment would feel the pinch, not to mention the loss of revenue to the travel industry because, as we all know, ecclesiastical executives have to travel a lot. There would be fewer church conventions, so hotels and restaurants in our great convention cities such as Miami and New York and Hawaii would be hurt. Taxing the churches could well trigger a depression or at least a recession.

Worse than this, though, would be the moral and social decline which would swamp us if the churches were taxed. Without preachers and churches to tell them how to behave, our young people would be demoralized. They wouldn't want to work and slave for money and status and all the benefits of the American way of life, but would go off somewhere and let their hair grow, and bathe infrequently, and prefer smoking pot to drinking martinis, and perhaps even indulge in sex before they are married. If enough of them fall into these evil ways they might organize and stage protests marches to clip the wings of the military-industrial complex which is so basic not only to our ideals but to our economy. And without the Church to teach them, how are they to understand the dogmas of the Trinity, and the virgin birth, and papal infallibility?

Our minds recoil in horror at the bleak prospects for our life and society were the churches to lose their tax-free status. Constantine gave it to the Church to do good, and the Church has done well. We must not let them take it away. We must fight. We must lobby. Perhaps we could join forces with Senator Long and others who have battled so valiantly to preserve the oil-depletion allowance. Our interests are parallel. The oil-depletion allowance is also a sacred American right, the elimination of which would bring on an unprecedented economic and spiritual collapse, as the oil industry has so clearly demonstrated to us.

THE BISHOP OF ROME BECOMES ASSISTANT EMPEROR

Constantine made another decision about this same time that was not designed for the Church's benefit, but as it turned out, it was. He moved his capitol to Constantinople. He said he liked the climate of Constantinople better than the climate of Rome, but his real reason was that Constantinople was situated more advantageously for keeping an eye on the whole empire.

With the emperor in Constantinople someone had to run things in Rome. The people of Rome began to look on the bishop of Rome as a sort of assistant emperor, and the bishop of course did nothing to discourage the idea. In those days it took a long time for calls to get through from Rome to Constantinople, almost as long as it does now. Somebody had to make decisions in Rome, so the bishop of Rome—who was supposed to be running only the Church—began to run everything down that way. Before long, if you wanted a variance to build an apartment house or a parking garage, or you wanted to complain about your garbage service, you had to go through the bishop's office.

Here we have the origin of the idea that a Christian bishop is entitled to secular as well as spiritual authority, a concept which is languishing somewhat in the modern world except in such areas as Spain and certain South American countries which have staunchly resisted the onslaughts of modern secularism. But the concept served the Church well in the expansion days of the corporation, and could even be revived to serve it again. Probably, too, the seizure of secular power by the bishop of Rome germinated the thought that eventually became the doctrine of the primacy of that office.

Another building block in the grand structure of the Christian Corporation was also mortised into place during this same period.

It had to do with the handling of heretics, and it arose as a consequence of another kindness from Constantine.

The emperor made a grant of cash to the clergy of North Africa, thinking that his benevolence would demonstrate to them on which side their bread was buttered. But Constantine had overlooked the fact that North Africa had two sets of Christian clergy. One was the standard-brand clergy loyal to the establishment. The other was the Donatist clergy, a bunch of pesky schismatics which we have already told you about.

CONTROVERSY OVER SINFUL BISHOPS

The Donatists claimed that the standard-brand bishop of North Africa had been ordained by a bishop who was said to have been in a state of sin at the time of the ordination, which he may have been for all we know. Anyway, you can't have a valid ordination when it is conducted by a bishop in a state of sin the Donatists said, and so they claimed the cash should go to them. Theirs was a specious argument, of course, and inasmuch as the regular Christians had the connections, the outcome was never in doubt. But the case is interesting because it demonstrated that the Church was beginning to think and act like a corporation.

First, it convened a conference to settle the theological issue involved. It met at Arles in Gaul, or France, and since we know that the outcome was quite predictable, we conclude, admiringly, that the conference was window dressing, good public relations. The conference settled the theological issue by voting that while it is better for a bishop not to be in mortal sin when conducting ordination, it is not always possible to ordain under ideal conditions, and thus the character of the bishop ordaining has nothing to do, one way or the other, with the validity of his ordinations, which seems to us the only sensible and realistic decision the Church could have made.

By affirming the validity of ordination by a sinful bishop the conference automatically made the Donatists heretics, because a heretic is anyone who deviates in his thinking from what is orthodox. Orthodox, of course, is whatever the establishment says it is.

The Donatists did not accept the decree in good grace, though, and kept pestering Constantine for a cut of the swag. This helped the true Christian Corporation to see that you can't be soft and easy with heretics, so it took out after the Donatists and closed down their churches and exiled several Donatist bishops, and some Donatists even got killed in the melee, all of which tended to cool things down somewhat. It also discouraged other greedy heretical groups from trying to divert Constantine's cash from flowing into the treasury of the true Christian Corporation.

PROPOSING AN OSCAR FOR CONSTANTINE

As a conscientious historian we must be objective and admit that not everyone shares our enthusiasm for Constantine and his contribution to the Christian Corporation. As we have already told you, no competent church historian other than ourself has much in the way of praise for the first Christian emperor. Avant-garde clerics, reformers, ecumenists, and renewalites who, like the poor, are always with us, want to minimize the institutional aspects of the Christian Corporation, and blame Constantine for making it a corporation in the first place.

Our evaluation is a stout vote of confidence in Constantine. We believe that if the Church ever gets around to awarding an Oscar for the greatest contribution to the Church it should go, somewhat posthumously of course, to Constantine. He isn't even a saint because to be made a saint there have to be miracles connected with your life or at least your tomb, and no one has reported any miracles connected with Constantine. But we think that granting the Church tax-free status is as much of a miracle as anyone could want. The very least the Church could do would be to make the date it became a legal corporation a major and obligatory feast day.

IV. *The council of Nicaea, the doctrine of the Holy Trinity, and some other stuff*

You would be hard put to find anyone who would deny that the most important of all Christian doctrines is the doctrine of the Holy Trinity. This doctrine describes for us with great exactitude just what God is like. Not everyone, however, is aware of how the Christian Corporation came into possession of this beneficent dogma, so we had better tell you about it.

Although the Christian Corporation up to the time of Constantine had been busy struggling to survive, as you have just read, it had not neglected the vital business of formulating a theology. In fact, it had formulated quite a number of theologies. We will now attempt to explain to you the theological situation just prior to the Council of Nicaea which, as you know, defined the dogma of the Trinity, but you will have to pay close attention.

COSMOLOGY AND SOTERIOLOGY EXPLAINED

In the early, intellectually crude days of the Christian Corporation, all you had to do to join it was to give assent to a simple statement of faith. But by the time the fourth century was well underway you had to decide whether you were fundamentally interested in cosmology or soteriology if you expected to have any standing at all in the Corporation. Cosmology, in case it has slipped your mind, is concerned with the nature of the universe. Soteriology is concerned with personal salvation. To put it another way, if you like to spend the evening looking at the moon you are a cosmologist. If you prefer attending a revival meeting you are a soteriologist.

Next, you had to decide to be either a Logos Christian, or a Modalist, or even worse, a Dynamic Monarchian. We could define these terms for you but it wouldn't help. You will recall, though, that by the time of Nicaea Logos Christianity had vanquished Modalism and even Dynamic Monarchianism, otherwise known as Adoptionism. Much theological progress had been made even before Nicaea, as you can readily see. However, despite the availability of many splendid answers to a vast variety of theological questions, there was a devout debate raging over the question, "Is Jesus to be thought of as God or as a man?"

We, of course, know the correct answer, contained as it is in the doctrine of the Holy Trinity as formulated at Nicaea and enshrined in the lucid, limpid language of the Nicene Creed. We would never dream of questioning it. We must be charitable, therefore, as we study some people who did question it. Remember, it wasn't actually evil to oppose Trinitarianism before Nicaea, as of course it would be today, because before Nicaea the Holy Trinity wasn't orthodox doctrine.

DOCTRINE OF TRINITY IMPROVES CHRISTIANITY'S OCTANE RATING

Had it not been for a theologian named Arius, who lived in Alexandria, the problem of the Holy Trinity might never have been settled and we would have had to struggle along without it. Christianity without the doctrine of the Trinity would be like gasoline without tetraethyl lead—an engine will run on leadless gas, but you get a lot more horsepower if you have some lead in it. Also, as we know from oil industry advertising, customers favor a gasoline that purports to contain complicated formulas which are beyond their comprehension but which sound impressive.[1] The Christian Cor-

---

[1] Some people point out that lead in gasoline pollutes the atmosphere, but we wouldn't want to carry our analogy of leaded gasoline and the doctrine of the Trinity this far.

poration discovered that its customers feel exactly the same way about theologies. This accounts for the perennial popularity of the doctrine of the Holy Trinity.

Arius said he had the answer to the question as to whether Jesus was a god or a man. The answer, he said, was that in one sense Jesus is just like God, but in another sense he isn't. This, said Arius, on the one hand makes him not quite god, but on the other hand not quite man either. It was best to think of Jesus as a *tertium quid,* he said. Many people said they found this explanation very helpful.

Arius went ahead to explain that he knew pious people liked to speak of Jesus as God, and he didn't mind them doing this so long as they didn't mean it. If they spoke of Jesus as God and actually meant it, though, that constituted blasphemy, Arius claimed, and the Church would have to do something about them such as excommunicate them. Arius' boss, a bishop named Alexander who was an ardent Trinitarian, responded by firing Arius.[2]

The anti-Arians, or Trinitarians, were thoroughly aroused by Arius' impudent doctrines, as well they should have been. Many dandy public debates were held between pro- and anti-Trinitarians, with large crowds attending. We are surprised that large crowds once attended theological debates because, regrettably, you couldn't get a baker's dozen to come to one today. What attracted the crowds back then wasn't so much the doctrinal dueling, because people then didn't understand what the theologians were talking about any better than people do today. What brought in the spectators was the spirited fighting which nearly always broke out at these affairs. The two teams of theologians and their supporters almost always resorted to fisticuffs and other forms of violence to prove who was right about the true nature of Christ. The crowd found this most entertaining.

---

[2] Both Arius and Bishop Alexander claimed an earlier theologian named Origen as their authority. A layman might think that one of them was lying, but they weren't. It is considered quite good form among professional theologians to quote the same authority to support opposite sides of a question.

CONSTANTINE'S THEOLOGICAL INADEQUACIES

The emperor, however, did not find it entertaining. Constantine had no trouble understanding the administrative problems of the Christian Corporation, but he was completely baffled by the theological disputes which kept many holy quarrels going full blast most of the time. We must not be critical of Constantine's theological insensitivity, though. Remember, he was a mere layman with little or no background in doctrine. True, he went so far as to call the Trinitarian dispute "an unprofitable question," which horrifies us until we recall that uninstructed laymen often fail to grasp the vital importance of finespun dogma.

What Constantine did grasp was that all this arguing was becoming politically divisive. He began sending messages to bishops and theologians saying, "Cut out the nonsense," and "don't you guys have enough to do without raising such a ruckus?" These messages did no good whatever, and the theologians went right on fighting each other with vigor and enjoyment.

Constantine then called a church council which was to meet at Nicaea, which as you know is in Bithynia, near Constantinople. This meant that Constantine wouldn't have to travel far to get to the council because he lived in Constantinople, but that some of the bishps and theologians were in for quite a trip. We doubt that the bishops from far away places minded the trip too much, though, because, as we have seen, by this time bishops traveled first class.[3] Constantine ordered the council to settle this theological dispute over the doctrine of the Holy Trinity, and also to decide on the right date for Easter.

The council was convened in May of the year A.D. 325. This is one of the most famous of all Christian dates because the Nicene Council was the first though not, some say unfortunately, the last ecumenical council.

The emperor himself came for the opening of the council, which was a lavish banquet for all the delegates. This set a precedent for

[3] They still do.

all future church councils, and even today any ecclesiastical con-
clave worth attending opens with a lavish banquet for all the
delegates. Technically, Constantine was ineligible to attend the council since he hadn't been baptized. However, the Christian Corporation
has always understood that the rules can be stretched some to
accommodate emperors and kings and movie stars. Constantine's
appearance was greeted with shouts and cheers of great enthusiasm.
We expect this was because of the high esteem in which the Corporation held the emperor, but some of it may have been due to
the fact that nobody could eat until Constantine arrived.

THE CLEVERNESS OF TRINITARIANS

After dinner, or maybe the next morning, the Arian or non-
Trinitarian party confidently submitted an Arian creed and moved
that it be made the normative test of whether you are an orthodox
Christian or a heretic. Everyone expected that a chap named Athanasius, who was the leader of the Trinitarian party, would immediately submit a Trinitarian creed, but he didn't. Instead, Eusebius of Caesarea,[4] who was sort of an Arian, but on the other
hand sort of a Trinitarian, so nobody was mad at him, stood up
and said he just happened to have on him a creed which he
thought everybody would like real well. Since it turned out to
have a very sweet sound when read out loud and was at the same
time beautifully indefinite on the theological points at issue, everyone said why not adopt it, and they did.[5]

We feel we should spare you the details of the debate which
followed, as trying to grasp the complexities of creedal arguments
can be most fatiguing to the mind. We shall, therefore, condense
the events at Nicaea to understandable proportions. The Trinitarians
never did submit their own creed. What they did was to submit
a succession of amendments to Eusebius' creed. By the time they

[4] Not to be confused with Eusebius of Nicomedia, a rabid Arian and therefore
a bad guy.
[5] Experience has shown that creeds which sound good but which nobody
can say exactly what they mean are the very best kind of creeds.

had finished, these amendments added up to saying that you had to believe God is three separate persons, and you also had to believe God is just one person, or you are a heretic.

How the Arians were persuaded to sign this creed we do not know, and it is too late to find out now. What the creed did was to say, in effect, that Arians were heretics. We suppose the Arians signed to cover their retreat before they were defrocked and sent to Siberia. Only a few Arians refused to sign, and they were defrocked and sent to Siberia.

THE PRINCIPLE OF CHRISTIAN THOUGHT CONTROL ESTABLISHED

The significance of Nicaea in the development of the Christian Corporation is that it established, for all time, the principle of Christian thought control as a right, privilege and duty of the Corporation. The Corporation does not refer to it as thought control, of course, but calls it by more felicitous names such as "protecting the purity of the faith." Whatever you call it, though, what happened at Nicaea makes it possible for the pope today to issue dogmas, and tell Corporation members of the Roman branch how to conduct their sex lives, and prohibit divorce, and pronounce on what is O.K. for the faithful to believe and what isn't. Since one of the Corporation's most attractive sales feature has proved to be its promise to do your thinking for you in matters of faith and morals, we are naturally terribly grateful to the Council of Nicaea for setting the precedent by which the Church relieves us of the time-consuming necessity for figuring out these things for ourselves.

Theologians assure us that it is awfully important for us to believe in the doctrine of the Holy Trinity, although they haven't explained exactly why. Theologians haven't explained the doctrine very clearly either. When you ask them to explain it, they say there is a mystery here. They hasten to add that all orthodox theologians have boasted, ever since the Council of Nicaea down to right now, that "in the doctrine of the Trinity both religion and philosophy came to highest expression," which is most reassuring.

We almost forgot to tell you that the Nicene Council also settled the date of Easter, which Constantine had told them to do. It settled on the first Sunday after the first full moon of the vernal equinox. This date combined Christian, Jewish and pagan practices, so nobody wanted to argue about it.

V. *The development of a style of Christian Corporation leadership after Nicaea—how the Bishop of Rome got to be Pope, and how administration won out over mysticism*

Modern Christians are fond of looking back on the early days of the Christian Corporation and sentimentalizing about them. "Those were the days, my friend," they often say, meaning that they imagine that back then everything about the Corporation was lovely and serene. It is our unpleasant duty to report that this is an illusion.

As we have seen, under Constantine the Church became a corporation in fact as well as in fancy. But its structure was sketchy at best, and as yet no clear style of Corporation leadership had emerged. There were bishops by this time, of course. But some were strong and some were weak. Some were soldiers and some were scholars. Some were administrators and some were mystics. Almost any kind of a person could be a bishop. There was no definitive profile of the Corporation executive such as we have today in a David Rockefeller or Henry Ford II.

You will recall that Constantine was hardly cold in his grave before the Germanic tribes began to pester the Roman Empire. The Goths, the Visigoths, the Ostrogoths, the Vandals, the Franks and others would come swooping down on various parts of the empire to the discomfort of everyone. Every so often they would sack Rome. The history of this period is studded with the names of such unpleasant personalities as Alaric, Ataulf, and Attila.

We usually think of these invasions of the empire by Huns and Barbarians as inimical to the best interests of the Christian Corporation, but in truth they were a tremendous help toward developing a style of leadership for the Corporation. Two facts we are apt to forget account for this. The first is that the headquarters of the Roman emperor was not at Rome but in Constantinople where Constantine had established it. The second is that some of these barbarian invaders anyway were already Christian[1] and would pay attention to the bishop of Rome. As historians tell us, these conditions provided a climate in which the political power of the bishop of Rome could be expanded with extreme rapidity.

Before all this, everyone agreed that St. Peter was the first bishop of Rome, and there was no denying that the Roman Church was the largest and richest church in the West, so the bishop of Rome had a lot in the way of prestige going for him. In addition, the Roman Church survived the Germanic invasions, and it was about the only institution to do so. But, in spite of all these credentials for the primacy of the Roman bishop there was nothing on paper to say that he was the number-one man of the Christian Corporation.

INNOCENT I APPROPRIATES APOSTOLIC TRADITION

How, then, did the bishop of Rome come to be universally recognized as the pope? Largely because the bishops of Rome began saying that naturally the bishop of Rome was the pope. Innocent I (402–417) claimed he was the official custodian of apostolic tradition, and if you are custodian of apostolic tradition it is hard for anyone else to say he is pope and make it stick.

Innocent also claimed that when the Council of Nicaea gave the bishop of Rome jurisdiction over trials of other bishops it confirmed the papal status of the bishop of Rome. Actually, the Council of

---

[1] Some of these barbarian Christians, especially the Vandals, were Arian Christians who did not accept the Nicene Creed and the doctrine of the Holy Trinity, so they weren't Christians by any meaningful definition of the term. About 493 Clovis, a Frankish heathen chieftain, married Clotilda, a genuine, non-Arian Christian, became a genuine, non-Arian Christian himself, and had his whole tribe baptized into the true Christian faith. A little later he swiped most of the Visigoths' territory and extended true Christianity to those parts, and before long the heresy of Arianism just petered out.

Nicaea never said this. It was the Council of Sardica, meeting some eighteen years after Nicaea, that said it. The Council of Sardica wasn't even a general council so what it said didn't impress anyone very much, which is why, we suppose, Innocent ascribed the action to Nicaea. However, it is a small matter, and we only bring it up to keep the record straight.

After Innocent, Leo I kept harping on the theme that St. Peter was primary among the apostles both in faith and in government, and that Peter bequeathed all this to his successors, although no will of Peter's has ever been found. Leo didn't just talk, though. He made his claims to primacy stand up pretty well because he had a well-equipped army. Then Pope Gelasius (492–496) wrote a letter to the emperor and said "there are . . . two by whom principally this world is ruled: the sacred authority of the pontiffs and the royal power. Of these the authority of the priests is so much the greater, as even for kings of men they will have to give an account in the divine judgment." This seemed reasonable to most people at the time. This was because they had been conditioned to view as reasonable anything the pope said. Here, then, we have the beginnings of the papacy, the idea of one headman for the Christian Corporation, although the concept was not completely firmed up until the middle ages.

The day-by-day operations of the Christian Corporation resided with the bishops, of course, But what does a bishop do? How does he operate? Should he be chosen for his piety or his practicality? What style of leadership should he affect?

Immediately after Nicaea there was no unanimity on the answers to these questions. We must remember that this was a young corporation. Its future markets were uncertain. It was still in the midst of the product-development phase of its operation. At this stage of any business some hesitancy and false steps are to be expected. Corporate bloopers are even to be expected from mature and successful businesses. We all recall that just a few years ago, the Ford Motor Company spent several hundred millions of dollars to give birth to the Edsel.

By a stroke of luck, two renowned bishops with widely differing styles of leadership were operating during the last twenty-five years of the fourth century. Thus, the Christian Corporation was able to observe from life rather than theorize as to what style was preferable.

ST. JOHN CHRYSOSTOM—A WEAK BISHOP

One of these men was named John. He operated in the Eastern division of the Corporation. As a young man he intended to be a hermit. However, not everyone is cut out to be a hermit, and John found that he wasn't.[2] So he went back to Antioch where he had been born and became a preacher.

Whatever criticisms we have of him as a leader—and we shall have some in a moment—there is no denying that he was a sterling preacher. His sermons, we are assured, were always "impeccably exegetical and eminently practical," a combination not easy to find in a preacher, then or now. People called him John *Chrysostom,* which means "John the Goldenmouth," and how many preachers can you find today whose congregations call them goldenmouth? Anyway, the name stuck, and today practically every literate Christian knows of St. John Chrysostom.

Chrysostom's sermons on love and marriage were, we are told, exceedingly well received.[3] We have an example of one of these sermons in which he said:

"You wives should never say to your husbands 'you lazy, good-for-nothing sluggard. Look at that man over there. He came up from nothing. He takes risks and makes voyages. He has made a fortune, and his wife wears jewels and goes out with a pair of milk-white mules.' "

Naturally all the husbands whose wives had been nagging them for a new pair of milk-white mules—which included most of the husbands, because milk-white mules were highly thought of by

---

[2] After he was hermit for a while, John became convinced that the life of a Christian bishop, while somewhat more comfortable than the life of a hermit, is "more heroic than sleeping in a rough bed and going without a bath." This is a point of view held by most bishops today, although very few, if any, modern bishops have personal experience with such privations.

[3] The Church felt then, and some branches still feel, that a celibate priest is best qualified to give advice on love and marriage.

the ladies of fourth-century Antioch—liked this kind of preaching very much, although we expect it irritated many of the wives.

However, before the wives could get too mad, Goldenmouth would say to the husbands in the congregation:

"If your wife does talk like this, say to her 'I could have married another wife with a better fortune and of a nobler family, but I picked you because I loved you, and because you are so modest and gentle.'"

Since husbands who get their wives milk-white mules are more numerous by far than husbands who can put out a line like this, we presume the wives got over being mad at Chrysostom and instead of nagging their husbands for milk-white mules began nagging them to talk like Goldenmouth said they should.

However, though a goldenmouthed preacher, Chrysostom was an administrative bungler. When he became bishop of Alexandria he kept haranguing the people to do something about the bad social conditions of the community, such as feeding the poor by sharing their own money and food with those who had none, an idea no more popular and no less radical then than it is today. Any good administrator knows that when you are bishop of Alexandria you do not condemn social conditions in Alexandria, just as George Wallace and Lester Maddox never criticize Alabama or Georgia but blast the mess in Washington and New York. The people of Alexandria complained that Chrysostom was giving their community a bad name. They didn't say he was wrong, because he wasn't. They just wanted him to shut up about it, much as Vice-President Agnew has suggested that our press and television industries strive to be more objective in their reporting and leave out the bad stuff.

He foolishly stirred up the clergy against him when he tried to impose on them chaste and abstemious habits of life along with conscientious attention to their duties. A bishop with an instinct for administration would have observed that the Alexandrian clergy consisted mostly of clerical sports who were not attracted to prayer and self-denial, and that a bishop who tried to reform them would incur their animosity.

Then he began to preach against the current styles in women's clothing. Now we do not mean to exclude feminine styles from the list of legitimate sermon topics. It has been a favorite of pulpiteers since the beginning of the Christian Corporation. In the hands of a canny preacher clever enough to condemn the styles—miniskirts, ample cleavage, for example—not suited to the ladies of his congregation, it can be a popular and quite harmless homiletical exercise. But what Chrysostom forgot was that the Empress Eudoxia was a member of his congregation, and she was the Jackie Kennedy Onassis of her generation, always turned out in the latest fad or fashion. The empress thought he was preaching at her, and understandably took offense, although we would guess that he wasn't preaching at her but just blowing off a little holy steam.

In no time at all, then, Chrysostom managed to alienate the empress, the middle-class establishment, and the clergy. He was popular only with the poor and the disinherited. No bishop, of course, should expect to survive on such slim support as this, and he didn't. He was exiled to a crossroads in Armenia called Cucusus, where they didn't have paved streets or inside plumbing. And the sad part is that he could have continued to bask in public favor in Alexandria except that he just never got the hang of administration.

HOW JESUS CAME TO BE BORN ON DECEMBER 25

About the only solid administrative accomplishment inherited from Chrysostom's reign as bishop was the fixing of the date for Christmas. The Corporation had been celebrating Jesus' birthday on January 6. But the pagans, who were numerous back then, had a competing festival on December 25. It was to mark the birthday of Mithras, the sun god. The Mithraic celebration was somewhat along the lines of Mardi Gras or the Oktoberfest, involving a lot of drinking and helling around. Regrettably, many Christians liked this celebration better than January 6, which was a good deal tamer in nature. Alarming numbers of Christians were dropping out of the Christian Corporation and taking up with Mithras just to get in on the celebration.

The Christian solution, arrived at by the solemn council of

bishops and promoted by Chrysostom, was to have a similar celebration on December 25, only call it Christian. To do this they needed an excuse similar to the birthday of Mithras, so they just said that Jesus was born on December 25. We now know that the correct date isn't December 25, because the birthday of Mithras is supposed to be on the shortest day of the year when the sun starts on its upward course, which is December 21. However, the Mithraites were working from a faulty calendar which claimed that December 25 is the shortest day of the year. By the time everything was straightened out, December 25 was universally acknowledged to be the correct date of Jesus' birth. The Christian Corporation wisely decided that it would be too confusing to change the date again. The Corporation also felt that it might be disturbing to the faithful to tell them they had been celebrating on the wrong day, so it didn't tell them.

We are glad to report that this administrative decision reversed the tide of Christians flowing into Mithraism, and, for all we know, helped proselytize many Mithraites for Christianity. It just shows the enormous importance of nimble administrative procedure, and demonstrates that Chrysostom could have been one of the administrative jewels in the crown of the Christian Corporation if he had only put his mind to it instead of concentrating on being a great preacher and social reformer.

AMBROSE THE ADMINISTRATOR

Let us now look at another famous bishop of the era. It is a much more heartening story. His name was Ambrose, and he operated in the Western division of the Christian Corporation. Ambrose was not a Christian. He was a Roman civil administrator serving as governor of Milan.

During his administration there was, in Milan, a war of unprecedented ferocity between the Arian Christians and the Trinitarian Christians. This was about fifty years after Nicaea had settled the question and pronounced Trinitarian Christians the only true Christians, so there shouldn't have been any fight at all at this late date.

But Arians don't give up easily. When the bishop of Milan died, the Arians plotted to run several Arian candidates for bishop hoping to best the Trinitarians.

Everyone knew that the election was going to be a mess, so Ambrose—who probably had no interest in the theological bickering —went to the church where the election was to be held to keep law and order between the fervent but contentious Christian factions. The church was packed, jammed and overflowing with Arians, Trinitarians, and candidates.

What happened next is one of the best-attested events in Christian history. In fact, we have three well-attested versions of the story, but the one we prefer goes like this: Ambrose went to the convention in the full regalia of his office, feeling that his unmistakable presence would act as a deterrent to the more violent forms of Christian expression often arising in these meetings. To achieve high visibility, he placed himself in the chancel, taking the most prominent seat he could find. Not being a Christian, he was no doubt unaware that this was the bishop's chair.

The meeting was rough and noisy. No one was maimed or killed, but the convention was hopelessly deadlocked, just as our Republican or Democratic conventions often are. With all the yelling and screeching no one could tell exactly what was happening. Then, a little kid in the back asked his dad to hold him up so he could see what was going on down front. When he saw Ambrose sitting in the bishop's chair, arrayed as he was in robes not unlike those of a bishop—only of course a bishop's robes are much finer and more costly than the robes of a governor, but we couldn't expect a little kid to know that—he shouted to his dad, "My God! They've elected Ambrose bishop," or something like that, the noise at the time being so great that we can't quote him word for word. When the people around him heard the words "Ambrose . . . bishop" they thought "Ambrose . . . bishop" had a nice sound to it, so they repeated it, and then people in the next row started saying it like a chant. Pretty soon the cathedral rang with the chant "Ambrose . . . bishop," and he was elected by acclamation.

THE FIRST PAGAN BISHOP

There was, of course, a small problem involved. Ambrose was duly elected bishop of Milan, but he wasn't even baptized, much less ordained. He did have the reputation of being moral, upright, just, kind, and many other things which we associate with being a Christian. So the Christian Corporation cut the red tape with a broad ax. Ambrose was baptized, ordained, run through all the lower grades of the clergy which you have to endure on your way to the top in the ecclesiastical race for success, and consecrated bishop—all in a week's time. This is by all odds the most spectacular climb in a clerical career in the history of Christendom.

Although we are inclined to consider such a procedure for selecting bishops as not to be recommended in every instance, in the case of Ambrose it worked out splendidly. Ambrose was adequate to superb in every talent and duty required of a bishop.

It was at preaching that Ambrose was "adequate," a judgment rendered by those who listened to him at the time. What it usually means when your parishioners say you are adequate as a preacher is that you are pretty bad but not out-and-out awful.

People think it is nice, too, if a bishop is a scholar, although being a scholar is by no means mandatory for a bishop. Ambrose distinguished himself as a scholar. He wrote so voluminously on theological subjects that the Christian Corporation still lists him as one of the "doctors of the church." A close inspection of his works reveal, however, that he copped most of his material, mainly from the Greek theologians. In ordinary or trade publishing this is called plagiarism and can get you in a mess of trouble if you get caught at it, but there is a churchly tradition that theologians are permitted to steal one another's stuff and it isn't plagiarism.

It was, however, as an administrator that Ambrose excelled. After all, he had been a government bureaucrat, and government bureaucrats are nearly always efficient, superb administrators. Ambrose knew how to run things. He knew which side of an issue to be

on at what time. He understood the administrative art of when to
be tough and crack down, and when to let up.

For example, he was smart enough to know that paganism had
had it in the Roman Empire. Give it a couple of good swift
kicks, he estimated, and it would expire. He gave it a couple of
good swift kicks and it did expire. Everyone said this was a great
victory for Christ, and Ambrose got credit for polishing off the
pagans.

He also decided that, from the administrative point of view,
the time had come to polish off the Arian Christians. The Empress
Justina was an Arian, and she asked Ambrose if the Arians couldn't
have just one church in Milan for Arians only, a church the
Trinitarians couldn't attend. This seems a reasonable request to us.
Milan was full of churches, and the Trinitarians would hardly
miss one. But Ambrose told the empress no, the Arians couldn't
have a church. The ability to make bold decisions such as this
is why Ambrose was a bishop and a brilliant administrator, and
you and I are not. He knew that the Arians would no sooner
have one church than they would want two churches, and so on,
and so on. He also knew that although sometimes you have to
compromise with heretics when they have a little muscle, the thing
to do when you've got them set up for the knockout is to let them
have it in the chops.

The empress was awfully upset by Ambrose's decision and said
if he wouldn't let her have a church, she would damn well take
one by force. So she rounded up some barbarian troops who were
Arian Christians and led them to the church of her choice with
full intent to capture it by force. But when they got there they
found Ambrose and a churchful of Trinitarian Christians singing
some Latin hymns which Ambrose had written. This scared the
barbarians, we don't know why, because the hymns surely couldn't
have been that bad. After all, Ambrose was reputed to be a
first-class hymn writer, and he is still called "the father of hymn
singing in the Latin language." Anyway, the empress gave up,
and that was pretty much the end of the Arian heresy in the
Roman Empire.

Ambrose is also famous for pushing the emperor around when the occasion called for it. One occasion that called for it was when the emperor, whose name was Theodosius, lost his temper and had his soldiers kill about seven thousand people who had displeased him. Normally it is unwise for the Christian Corporation to be at odds with the political corporation. Careful, administratively sound bishops usually go to great lengths to avoid giving offense to emperors and kings and presidents. But if popular opinion is running against the political establishment for some unwise policy or action, then it can be advantageous for the Christian Corporation to challenge the political corporation.

This is what Ambrose did. He ordered the emperor to do public penance for his sins, something emperors seldom wish to do. But Theodosius just about had to do it, and he did. By forcing the emperor to submit to the bishop, Ambrose greatly strengthened the Christian Corporation, because people secretly like to see their leaders humbled every now and then, and much admire whoever does the humbling.

The perceptive reader is now in a position to make a comparison between two contrasting styles of leadership in the Christian Corporation. Chrysostom and Ambrose both lived at the same time. Both were bishops. Both had their troubles with the political establishment. But whereas Chrysostom bungled almost every opportunity and ended up in exile and disgrace, Ambrose went from victory unto victory, and ended up revered by all and full of honors.

Why did Ambrose win and Chrysostom lose?

The reason is ridiculously easy to see. Chrysostom majored in asceticism and preaching, and mysticism. He was an acknowledged star at all three. But he never understood the principles of administration and corporation management.

Ambrose, on the other hand, was no great shakes as a preacher, and he left no monuments in the fields of mysticism and asceticism. But he was an administrator worthy of being president of Standard Oil or Ling Tempco Vaught. One is pressed to think of a nicer compliment.

The contrast was not lost on the early Christian Corporation.

The Church did not miss the lesson here, to wit, mystics are losers, while administrators are winners when it comes to corporation leadership. From this time on the Christian Corporation made a conscientious effort to select only capable administrators to be bishops, and this accounts for most of the Corporation's success.

VI. *St. Anthony invents monasticism and solves a crisis in the Christian Corporation*

The story of the Christian Corporation after Nicaea is a thrilling tale of growth and progress, with a minor setback here and there—the kind of problems any corporation perforce must cope with. In 361 Julian, a dedicated pagan, became emperor. He tried to turn back the clock and convert all the Christians to paganism. But the empire was too far gone in Christianity and it didn't work. Fortunately, Julian went on a campaign against the Persians in the second year of his reign and didn't come back. He was the last heathen emperor of Rome. After Julian the Christians had no real opposition.

Corporations which have a monopoly on their line of business, though, do have the problem of keeping everyone on their toes and working like mad for the good of the corporation. To put the Christian Corporation's problem in perspective, after Constantine made it socially acceptable and politically advantageous to be a Christian, there was an influx of what we would call nominal Christians into the Church. A nominal Christian is one who, for whatever reasons, wants to be identified with the Church but is not terribly enthusiastic about it. What you had, then, was a congregation which was a mixed bag of serious and not so serious members. For purposes of clarity let us refer to the serious members as platinum-plated Christians, and the not so serious or nominal members as tin-plated Christians. Although all comparisons are odious, and this one is certainly invidious, we want to make it clear that the comparison is not ours. It was made by the platinum-plated Christians. Their solution to the problem was to kick all the tin-plated Christians out of the Church and have it as an institution just for platinum-plated Christians.

THE TIN-PLATED CHRISTIANS VANQUISH THE PLATINUM-PLATED CHRISTIANS

This was not done. One reason it was not done was that in every congregation the tin-plated Christians vastly outnumbered the platinum-plated Christians,[1] and the pastors would not hear a plan which would decimate their membership rolls and cut off so many fine contributors to the budget.

Naturally, the standards of Christian behavior observed by the tin-plated Christians was somewhat more relaxed than that of the platinum-plated group. As long as all Christians believed the world was coming to an end soon, most Christians conducted themselves with pious decorum. But after a few generations and the world was still whipping along, it became increasingly difficult to convince many of the members that the end was near. Consequently Christian standards of conduct degenerated alarmingly, as people behave at their best only when they are scared not to.

As the Christian Corporation noted the tendency of some of its customers to lose ground in the race of suffering and self-denial, it came up with an ingenious solution. First, Bishop Kallistos, who was bishop of Rome and presumably the pope, said that while it was true that the Church contained some members whose conduct was defective, this was O.K. because Noah's Ark had on board "things clean and unclean," which cleared up the problem.

Then the Church said that people had fallen into the bad habit of thinking of the Church as a community of saints, but that it wasn't this at all. What it was, it said, was an "agency of salvation." We can, of course, see the wisdom of this distinction. While a community of saints is a very pretty self-image, it seldom conforms to reality. Also, an agency of salvation is just another way of

[1] They still do.

saying that the Church is fundamentally a corporation. A community of saints has practically no growth potential and a very limited appeal. It cannot sell indulgences or finance cathedrals or struggle with princes and emperors for secular power, whereas an agency of salvation can.

The next step in the solution to this corporation crisis was to declare that there are two recognizable and acceptable grades of Christians. All Christians, the Corporation said, are obligated to adhere to the Christian "requirements." The Christian requirements weren't too tough on you, and nearly anybody could follow them with a minimum of inconvenience.

But, as Hermas had said, a man can do more than is required of him if he feels like it. He can follow the Christian "advice," and this will pay an enormous stock dividend in heaven. The Christian advice was centered around the scriptural admonition to sell all you have and give it to the poor, and about becoming "eunuchs for the kingdom of heaven's sake." Becoming a eunuch for any reason doesn't attract too many people, but in this case you didn't have to become a eunuch in fact. It only meant that you had to behave as if you were one.

The dividing of Christians into two grades elicits our admiration. It is obvious to us that not everyone wants to give up sex and money. How glad we are that the Christian Corporation ruled that you don't have to give up sex and money or such outstanding Christian families as the Kennedys would be excluded from membership in the Corporation.

On the other hand, those who yearn to be platinum-plated Christians and earn a truly enormous return, such as the very best accommodations in paradise, on their spiritual investment are also provided for.

If you are puzzled by this arrangement, think of these Christians as a modern professional football team. You have to be good to make the team at all. However, every pro team has its stars who get the big money and the publicity as well as its less talented and lesser-known players. The platinum-plated Christians were the Joe Kapps and the Roman Gabriels of the Christian Corporation. The tin-plated Christians were the anonymous linemen and journey-

men backs, very necessary to the team but who do not merit a
star's paycheck. This little explanation should enable you to understand why the Christian Corporation established the distinction between platinum-plated and tin-plated members.

It was the monastic movement which organized suffering and
self-denial, offering platinum-plated Christians an attractive method
for practicing the Christian "advice."

Everyone knows that it was St. Anthony of the Desert who
invented monasticism. A careful scrutiny of the records shows us
that Origen, well before Anthony, lived a sort of monastic life.
Nor must we forget the Order of the Holy Virgins[2] who were much
in evidence in the Church in the third century. To be honest,
before Anthony came on the scene there was a thriving movement
which can best be described as "You, too, can be a monastic,
even if you are married, without leaving home." We don't know
precisely how this style of monasticism worked, but we can imagine.
There were also monastics among the heathen religions of India,
Greece, and Egypt, and among the Jews prior to Anthony. But
these are minor blemishes in Anthony's title of inventor of monasticism.

The idea behind monasticism is delightfully simple. Its appeal is
almost exactly the same as that of the banks trying to get you to
join their Christmas savings club. Deny yourself all year and stash
away your money, the banks urge, so that come Christmas you can
indulge in a wild spending spree. A monastic operates on the
assumption that if he denies himself, and suffers, and mortifies
the flesh, and undergoes privation in this present world, he is bank-
ing huge chunks of heavenly currency which can be used for a
perpetual Christmas in eternity. The best way to coin this spiritual
cash, according to accepted monastic practice, was to deprive the
body of food, sleep, sex, and baths,[3] which gives you an idea of
what people in the third century considered fun.

---

[2] There is, apparently, a significant difference between Holy Virgins and
ordinary virgins, but we have been unable to discover exactly what this
difference is.

[3] The reason the original monastics lived alone in the desert is probably
because if you had very many of these unwashed saints living together in a
house, the atmosphere would tend to get pretty gamy.

We know from the Jacobite Arabic synaxary that Anthony was born in the village of Heptanomus, or in a village in the monarchy of Nohuit. Anyway, he was born in Egypt. Egypt at this time was a part of the Roman Empire. The Egyptians didn't care much for the Roman emperors, who had kicked the Ptolemies out of Egypt. The Egyptians hadn't cared much for the Ptolemies either, so they were pretty philosophical about the whole thing.[4]

During Anthony's early years the Romans, who weren't doing too well economically, kept pestering the Egyptians to send them more food and taxes which, historians say, had a depressive effect on the spirits of the Egyptians. This may explain Anthony's somewhat pessimistic view of the world.

ANTHONY DROPS OUT OF SQUARE SOCIETY

St. Anthony's parents were rather well-to-do, but Athanasius in his biography of Anthony says that the future saint didn't care too much for his folks.[5] Here we have an important clue to Anthony's personal hang-ups. He was a middle-class, privileged kid who rejected his parents and their values, and dropped out of square society. We could almost say he was the prototype of today's hippie, what with his unshorn hair, aversion to bathing, and living in the open, except that we are told that the modern hippie is more permissive about sex than St. Anthony was. Anyway, Athanasius candidly admits that Anthony wasn't too broken up when the old folks passed on to their reward because he was anxious to get on with being a drop-out in the desert and looked on family ties as a handicap in the race for holiness.[6]

Anthony started out by becoming an apprentice hermit to some

---

[4] What they said was that one set of crooks had supplanted another set of crooks. But third-century Egyptians are famous for their cynicism.

[5] They wouldn't let him go to the village school and learn Greek. However, since there is no indication that Anthony wanted to learn Greek, this can't be the reason he didn't like his parents.

[6] Anthony had a younger sister, and Anthony's father had made him promise to bring her up and take care of her. But when the folks died he chucked her in an orphanage, because you can't be a good hermit with a kid sister tagging along.

nameless old man who lived in the desert and who had long experience in the subtleties of self-denial. He would put out a small meal for Anthony when Anthony was starving. Then he would only permit him to eat half of it. He would also make Anthony get up every three hours and chant a psalm nine times. Chanting a psalm nine times every three hours, especially when you are hungry and sleepy, may seem pointless to us, but for a hermit it is just like daily blocking and tackling practice to a football team. It toughens the spiritual muscles.

There were quite a few ascetics living in the desert during Anthony's apprentice years, and Anthony would go visit all of them and pick up tips on how to be a hermit. Each of these hermits was a specialist. One would specialize in fasting. Another was awfully good at exhausting the body. Another had learned how to develop himself spiritually by getting along with practically no water. All this was invaluable to Anthony in training for his chosen profession.

We are told that his first weeks as a hermit "seemed (to Anthony) like a long honeymoon." The devil, though, doesn't give up that easily. First, he put thoughts into Anthony's head about how nice it would be to cut out all this nonsense and go home to a good meal and a clean bed. Though the idea was appealing, Anthony fought off the temptation.

Then the devil brought up his big guns. He filled Anthony's head with visions of dancing girls and other erotica. Here we have a genuinely first-class temptation. We, of course, are exposed to this sort of thing every day through television and the movies and the lingerie ads, not as temptations to sin, but for the worthy purpose of moving the merchandise, which makes it perfectly acceptable. But the devil was up to no good when he sent a particularly alluring vision to Anthony, say the early Egyptian equivalent of Raquel Welch or Mamie Van Doren. Anthony, who knew that all women are bad business, and that dancing girls are especially inhibitive of the spiritual life, would then roll around in the hot sand and get stuck with sandburrs and little sharp rocks, and contrive to get himself covered with bugs which bit him pretty good. Then the wicked, lascivious visions would float on by, because it is most difficult to retain voluptuous images while being scorched and gouged and bitten.[7]

According to biographers the devil made one last stab at corrupting Anthony. He came to visit Anthony in the form of a little black boy and said, "I am the spirit of fornication." Exactly what the devil had in mind by this trick the biographers do not tell us. But a fellow who has resisted bevies of strip-teasers should have no difficulty with a second-rate temptation such as this, and Anthony didn't. He kicked the devil out in no time and without a second thought. Then he went to tell some of his ascetic buddies how he had resisted all these attractive temptations. His buddies, mightily titillated by Anthony's account of all those concupiscent cuties, replied in chorus, "How beautiful are the feet of him who walks in the light."[8]

After living in a little hut for a while, Anthony thought it was time to exercise the principle of upward mobility, which hermits normally do by moving to a new address in the desert. So he found an old tomb and took up residence. This sounds kind of creepy to you and me, but according to the values esteemed by recluses a tomb is a step up from a hut. Besides, hermits don't mind creepy places.[9] There was a bunch of little devils living in the tomb, and these imps looked on Anthony as a squatter. They took to beating up on him, leaving him black and blue and pretty sore. When this didn't drive him out they made an awful racket every night, but as Anthony didn't sleep much anyway, he was only mildly annoyed.

However, ascetics consider it good monkish practice to move every now and then, so after a while Anthony left the tomb and found an old abandoned fort. The fort afforded more room in which to practice his austerities. Also, it had a stream running through it, which meant that Anthony had at last moved into a home with

---

[7] Modern spiritual manuals recommend frequent cold showers to quell concupiscent urges, but cold showers are impractical if you are living in the desert.

[8] Where Anthony had been walking, of course, was in the desert, so his feet were probably pretty dirty. We must, remember, then, that it is the sentiment rather than the reality that counts in statements such as this.

[9] One hermit moved into a tomb and found a mummy's head on the floor, which he appropriated and used for a pillow.

running water, a genuine status symbol then as well as now, although since he didn't bathe, and limited himself to maybe half a cup of water a day for drinking purposes, it is not clear to us what advantages a home with running water had for Anthony. There were also a lot of snakes living in the fort, but when Anthony moved in the snakes moved out, so he must have smelled pretty strong, even for snakes.

Before too long, Anthony gained a reputation as a super-monk. Other ascetics, hoping that by propinquity to the acknowledged number-one man of their profession some of his sanctity would rub off on them, pitched their tents around Anthony's fort. Before long there was a thriving community of hermits around Anthony, and that is how the idea of a monastery got started, although a hermit is supposed to live in solitude, and therefore the idea of a monastery is a contradiction in terms.

THE MONASTIC MOVEMENT ORGANIZED

Anthony ended up building a couple of monasteries because of popular demand, but he wasn't especially enthusiastic about the project because he was a born loner.[10] It wasn't until a fellow named Pachomius, a lad of twenty, resigned from the army and became a monk, that the monastery movement bloomed. No doubt the splendid administrative training he received in the army enabled him to see that you have to organize something if it is ever to amount to anything. So he established what is officially considered to be the first bona fide Christian monastery. This was at a place called Tabennisi, which is in southern Egypt, or was then, around A.D. 315. The monastery brought to suffering and self-denial a sense of organization, with rules and regulations and a strict schedule. It also had a headman who told everyone what to do and no back

---

[10] If you wonder how Anthony got so much done in one lifetime, we are pleased to report that he lived to be one hundred years old. Even at the age of a hundred, so Athanasius tells us, he still had all his teeth. It seems unlikely to us that a chap who never ate anything but a little bread and water and salt once a day—hardly a balanced diet—and there is no record of him taking vitamin shots either, could live so long, let alone keep his teeth. But who are we to doubt Athanasius?

talk.[11] Before long he had a chain of ten monasteries going. Seeing no reason why women couldn't get in on a good thing so long as they weren't around the men, he invented the nunnery or convent, although it wasn't called a nunnery or convent until much later.

At this point in history, then, the Christian Corporation was able to offer those who aspired to follow the Christian "advice" and become platinum-plated Christians, two distinct options. One could choose the hermitic, or eremitic form of suffering and self-denial and go it alone. Or if you preferred to mortify the flesh as a part of a group you could be a cenobite and join a monastery or convent. The offering of options is always good corporate practice, as our modern automobile manufacturers have discovered. But it can be expensive. The Christian Corporation soon saw that it was better for the Corporation if ascetics could mostly be organized into ascetic communities, and though the eremitic form of Christian endeavor persisted for a time, progress was clearly on the side of the cenobites.

It was a case of the eremites being an individually manufactured, hand-tooled product, whereas the cenobites were shaped by the assembly-line process. Hand-tooled products are very fine, of course, but they simply can't compete with the assembly line. Look at what happened to the Pierce-Arrow and the Duesenberg.

Athanasius, Anthony's old pal, introduced the monastery into the Western division of the Christian Corporation, which up to that time had had to struggle along the rocky road to sainthood without benefit of either eremites or cenobites. The Western division knew how to carry the ball though, once it got hold of it, a lot better than the Egyptians.[12] Originally, the monastic movement was for laymen. Before long, though, the officers of the Christian Corporation saw that monasticism had splendid possibilities for organizing the clergy. When Benedict of Nursia put down his famous rules for running a monastery along military lines, the Order of

---

[11] The headman of a monastery is called an abbot. Pachomius chose himself as abbot of Tabennisi, which is why he was the first Christian abbot.
[12] Egyptians have a lot of big ideas, but they don't always carry them out as well as they might.

Benedictines, which has done so much for the world, not the least being their manufacture of a famous and delicious form of booze, was born. From that time on the monastic movement became increasingly clerical in nature.

THE CONTRIBUTIONS OF THE EREMITES

It would be wrong if, in our enthusiasm for the cenobitic form of monastic life, we neglected to cite the immense contributions of the eremites. It was the eremites, for example, who developed the custom of holding contests to see which eremite could endure the most hardship and privation.[13] In a typical eremite tournament the monks would stand on one leg like a stork. The last man to faint was adjudged the winner and therefore the holiest. There were eremites such as the famous and celebrated Simeon Stylites who lived for years on top of a pole, certainly not the easiest of holy privations to endure.

The eremites were also awfully good at avoiding contact with women, which isn't easy in any age. Some eremites imposed on themselves a rule that they would never even look at a woman. We have a picture from this period of church history which shows a group of women visiting a holy hermit. He has his eyes covered with his hands so as to keep his vow, although he is peeking at the girls through his fingers. However, we doubt that this was a very serious sin, entailing no more than a brief sojourn in the more comfortable suburbs of purgatory before being admitted without prejudice through the portals of heaven.

We would think that monasticism would have a limited appeal, but to our amazement it grew like crazy almost from the time St. Anthony invented it. However, the hippies and the yippies grew like crazy almost from the time they were invented, and no one can figure out their appeal either, so we shouldn't worry about it. Originally thought of by the Corporation as a convenient vehicle for particularly zealous Christians who wanted to follow the Chris-

---

[13] Cenobites were not eligible to complete in these contests. For skill in hardship and privation, cenobites are not classed in the heavyweight division with eremites.

tian "advice" instead of merely fulfilling the Christian "requirements," it soon became apparent that monasticism was a marvelously flexible device. It could be used to organize missionary activity. It was a source of cheap agricultural labor. A well-disciplined order could be employed to mount a vigorous campaign to snuff out heresy. Many monasteries learned to make superb wine. Once it grasped the potential of the monastic movement the Christian Corporation hastily sought to make it a subsidiary, which it pretty much did, and few subsidiaries have done so much for the parent body as the monastic movement has done for the Christian Corporation, as we shall see in future chapters.

VII. *The organizational structure of the Christian Corporation takes shape*

We saw, in an earlier chapter, how the young, unorganized church decided to have a headman in each congregation who was called the bishop. But how did this purely local office evolve into the powerful, administratively oriented, honors-filled position a bishop occupies today?

In those days most Christians lived in cities. As the Church grew, there would be several congregations meeting in the same city. This is not so very different from the situation today where in an ordinary city we will have from five to ten Methodist churches, and three or four Presbyterian churches, and a couple of Episcopalian churches,[1] and heaven knows how many Baptist churches (there are so many brands of Baptists and they spring up so rapidly).

There was a difference between the early city congregations and ours, though. In our system each church is a separate congregation even from others of the same denomination. Back then, all congregations in a city considered themselves to be part of one Christian community, or in reality, one congregation. We can illustrate how this worked by reference to St. Paul's letter to the Church at Rome. It was supposed to have been read to the Church, and in our imagination we see it being read to one big, impressive

---

[1] One for the top layer of society, and another one for the couple of layers just below the top layer. Sometimes there is also an Episcopalian mission for those layers of society to which the other two churches wouldn't care to cater.

congregation. The Church at Rome, though, was not one vast body but dozens of small congregations scattered all over the city. Thus it was probably necessary to have St. Paul's Epistle to the Romans xeroxed so each individual congregation could have a copy to read aloud.

A modern example of what the Church at Rome was like in makeup would be the Chicago Democratic party, which is composed not of one vast assembly but of hundreds of ward and precinct organizations and unified by a common purpose. In the case of the Chicago Democrats, the common purpose is to do exactly what Mayor Daley tells them to do, so his function is similar to that of the bishop in the Church at Rome.

Now, to the evolution of the office of bishop. It was assumed that the bishop of Rome, or wherever, was bishop of all the individual groups of Christians in his city. You can see that as the number of individual congregations grew so did the stature and importance of the bishop, administrative prestige in either sacred or secular corporations being directly linked to the size and wealth of whatever the administrator is administering. It was also the bishop's job to start new churches, but when a city has all of the churches it can reasonably support you have to look for new territory. So the bishops would send deacons and presbyters[2] out into the surrounding villages to found new churches, and these churches were considered a part of the bishop's responsibility. It was, then, by natural process of growth in the Christian Corporation that the job of bishop kept getting better and better, and more to be desired.

The growth of the Christian Corporation also improved the status, finances, and prospects of the ordinary clergy. In the early days of the Corporation you could hardly tell the clergy from the laity, but the Corporation soon saw that this would never do. A corporation, by its very nature, must have a hierarchical executive structure. Without an executive pyramid to climb, you not only kill individual initiative, but no one knows who is boss over whom.

---

[2] Deacons and presbyters were what today we would call assistant pastors.

THE SEVEN-LAYER PYRAMID

The clerical pyramid, developed early, had seven distinct levels. Bishops, of course, were first, or on top. Then came presbyters, then deacons. These were the major orders. There were then four minor orders descending in importance from acolyte to exorcist to reader to janitor. Exorcists were supposed to be skilled in driving out evil spirits. We can't be precise about what acolytes and readers did, but janitors did then about what janitors do now, only back then janitors had to be ordained, and now they don't.[3]

One of the first items a growth corporation must attend to is the establishment of procedures for handling money. When the bishop was just the head of one little congregation there wasn't much money to worry about, so he handled all financial affairs as he saw fit. He paid himself what he thought he was worth. He paid the other clergy what he thought they were worth.

After Constantine made the Church a legal corporation which could receive tax-exempt gifts, the cash flow increased enormously. It was decided that to protect the bishop from temptation to the sin of greed it would be best to have a formal rule for splitting the take. The rule was that church income was to be divided into four equal parts—one part for the bishop, naturally; one for all the other clergy in the area under the bishop; one part for upkeep of buildings and providing services; and one part for the poor. This seems an equitable arrangement to us, although we do come across records of complaint that inasmuch as the bishop's share came off the top, and since his bookkeepers handled the division, sometimes the bishop's equal share was somewhat larger than, say, the equal share for the poor.[4]

[3] There is some holdover of the ancient custom of ordained janitors, though. Today, many small churches too poor or too cheap to hire a janitor will often let the preacher sweep out and build fires and perform other janitorial duties.
[4] You never hear such a complaint against a bishop today, but oddly enough, you frequently hear it leveled at heads of modern secular corporations. Every stockholders' meeting has at least a few angry protests that the chairman and president and other officers of the corporation are reducing profits by paying themselves far too much.

HOW THE PARISH SYSTEM IMPROVED CHURCH FINANCES

It wasn't until the sixth century that the parish system as we know it today came into popular use. Under this system, in which a priest is in charge of all the Christians in a prescribed area and a bishop has many local priests under his jurisdiction, the priest would collect all the money he could, keep two-thirds of it, and send one-third of it to the bishop. As you can see, this schedule reduced the share of income given to the poor to zero per cent. However, we mustn't be too critical of this arrangement. Remember that by the sixth century the Christian Corporation was expanding rapidly and thus was involved in expensive building programs, booming missionary campaigns, plus bearing the burden of escalating administrative costs. It was comparable to the present situation with our own national government. Our leaders have had to face the fact that we can't afford an expensive war in Vietnam to enhance our national honor and for other worthy if sometimes obscure purposes and at the same time carry on a full complement of benevolent programs. So we have been forced to cut back on welfare, hunger and education relief, along with cancer research, public housing, and many fine but not essential projects. And anyway, the local priest was supposed to give a little something to the poor out of his two-thirds cut, which we presume he did.

We have now observed how the Christian Corporation, starting as a minuscule, disorganized religious group had—by the sixth century—emerged as a large and viable institution with hierarchical leadership patterns and sound corporate financial structure. It was more durable if not yet so powerful as the political corporation. An amazing story indeed! But this is only the beginning. Let us hasten to the next chapter and learn how the young, vigorous Christian Corporation expanded its markets into what was to become the English-speaking world, and thus ensured that the whole Western Hemisphere would ultimately be Christian.

VIII. *How the first great Pope nailed down England for the Christian Corporation*

As we have seen, there were some able popes in the fifth century—notably Innocent I and Leo I. But the first pope to merit the title "Great" was Gregory I. He is more familiar to us as Gregory the Great. It was not until Gregory that the Christian Corporation had a man at the helm comparable in wisdom, business acumen, and bold action to a J. Pierpont Morgan or Cornelius Vanderbilt.

Gregory came along at the tail end of the sixth century. Although he began his career in the Christian Corporation as a monk, he soon discovered that his own temperament was "too active for the cloister."[1] Once he got out of the cloister and into the real world of business and politics, he churned out achievements at such a pace that we can't possibly list them all. We will tell you about a few of them, though, beginning with the least important and going to the most important.

By no means negligible, but certainly not vital to his ultimate greatness, Gregory is remembered as a systematic theologian of some renown. In fact, like Ambrose of whom we read a few pages ago, he still carried the title of "Doctor of the Church."

---

[1] Gregory was very fond of monasticism, though, and continued to recommend it for other people because he thought it would be good for them.

GREGORY I SHOWS US THE PROPER PERSPECTIVE ON SEX

As a theologian he was a disciple of Augustine of Hippo. He improved on Augustine no little, though, by adding a lot more miracles and angels and more emphasis on the devil than Augustine had, and Augustine had plenty. He also showed us more clearly than anyone before him how awfully dirty sex is. He demonstrated beyond any reasonable doubt that it is the disgusting act of conception which is responsible for us being fettered in original sin. We might have gone right on copulating and thinking it just good fun if Gregory hadn't told us differently.

We also owe to Gregory the systematic theologian the doctrine of purgatory. He didn't exactly invent it. It had been hanging around on the fringes of Christian theology for some time as a likely idea. But Gregory said it was a certainty, although he didn't tell us how he arrived at this conclusion. He said that from then on the faithful were to believe that "there is a purgatorial fire before the judgment for certain light sins." We all know, of course, how the doctrine of purgatory has enriched Christian theology, but not many of us knew that Gregory was the one responsible for it.[2] Gregory also advanced the idea of the treasury of the saints. The way this works, if your own moral credit on the heavenly books or computer is a bit short of the amount required for salvation, it is possible—usually by paying earthly cash to the Christian Corporation—to borrow from the good works of the saints who, of course, piled up many more moral and spiritual merits than one person needs to get safely inside the pearly gates. The treasury of the saints, then, is sort of like salvation insurance—a wise investment and a great comfort to policyholders.

As if these were not scholarly accomplishments enough, Gregory also wrote the *Moralia,* which isn't what you would think it is, but is an exposition on the Book of Job. He also wrote *Regula*

---

[2] The doctrine of purgatory has also enriched the Christian Corporation, as without any purgatory to get your relatives out of, no one would pay for indulgences and prayers for the dead.

Pastoralis, a handbook on how to get ahead in the ministry, and *Dialogues on the Life and Miracles of the Italian Fathers.* Some critics consider *The Dialogues* overly credulous, but we think it is a charming work.

However, Gregory did not come to be called "Great" because he was an outstanding theologian, important as that may be. The Christian Corporation has never lacked for competent systematic theologians. The libraries overflow with their writings, and they are still grinding them out. What is rare, though, are truly brilliant administrators. As we saw in a previous chapter, the Corporation —after Chrysostom and Ambrose—put itself squarely on the side of administration as the indispensable requirement for church leadership. Sometimes the Corporation will make an intellectual a bishop or even a cardinal (the case of John Henry Newman comes to mind), but it never lets them run anything more important than a college or a choir school.

No one disputes that Gregory was the outstanding administrator developed by the Christian Corporation up to his time, and one of the Corporation's all-time stars in this department.

Gregory started out his reign by raising his own army and conquering the Lombards. Then he reaffirmed the principle of the primacy of Peter's see, or that the bishop of Rome is number one. When you have your own well-equipped army it is much easier for everyone to accept the legitimacy of a claim like this than it is when you are just talking.[3]

What shows us that Gregory had a genuine instinct for administration, though, is that he was ever alert to expand the Christian Corporation by moving into new territories. Constant expansion of markets is a hallmark of every successful corporation.

Now let us set the stage for our story of how Gregory got the idea for expanding into the British Isles.

---

[3] Gregory did have a little trouble with the Patriarch of Constantinople, John the Faster, who billed himself as "universal bishop," but nothing ever came of it.

GREGORY GETS A GREAT IDEA FROM SOME SLAVES

Gregory—who, good Christian that he was—would often go down to the slave market in Rome. He liked to talk to the slaves. He also liked to pick up a bargain when one was to be had, because the Christian Corporation in those days owned a lot of real estate, just as it does today, and needed plenty of slaves to work the land.

One day Gregory heard that a fresh shipment of slaves of a brand not often available had arrived in the market. He went down immediately to inspect the merchandise. These slaves, he saw, had yellow hair, blue eyes, and very light skin color. Gregory was much taken with them.

"Where are you from?" he asked them.

"From Deira," they replied. Gregory, an educated man, knew that Deira was the name for the western part of Yorkshire. Then one of the slaves added gratuitously, "We are of a race called Angles."

"You look like angels to me," Gregory replied, leading us to suspect that he had an unfortunate predilection for the pun as a form of humor.

"All angels should be Christians," Gregory continued, "so I shall go myself to the kingdom of Deira and save your people *de ira.*" We don't know if these slaves knew that *de ira* is Latin for "from the wrath of God," but of course we know it, and it confirms our suspicion that Gregory couldn't resist a pun.

When Gregory consulted his calendar he discovered there was no block of time available to him sufficiently long for a missionary journey to Deira. But he didn't forget his promise. The papal archivist or some research assistant turned up the information for him that Britain had been Christianized very early in the history of the Church—so early that no one had any records as to who had actually done the Christianizing. Then the Roman legions, which were an essential part of early missionary programs just as British colonial forces were so essential to missionary programs in the nineteenth century, got tired of the climate and went home to

Rome. The legions left a vacuum into which the heathen Angles and Saxons moved with alacrity. The Angles and the Saxons were an uncouth lot, as we know from the popular Anglo-Saxon words still in use today.[4] They drove the good Christian Britons into the mountains of Wales, took over the country, and practiced disgusting pagan rites.

Since Gregory couldn't go himself to Britain, he found a monk named Augustine, later called Augustine of Canterbury to distinguish him from Augustine of Hippo, and told him to take forty other monks and go convert the Angles and the Saxons.

Augustine's intrepid little band started out in high spirits. But when they got to France they began to hear horror tales of what the Angles and the Saxons were like. So they stopped and wrote a letter to Gregory saying maybe this was not a propitious time to save England, so could they please come home? But Gregory was a brave man as well as a decisive administrator. He wrote them by return mail to catch the first boat for England. They arrived in England sometime in A.D. 597.

Saving England wasn't actually too difficult. Queen Bertha, whose husband was King Ethelbert of Kent, was already a Christian, having been brought up in Paris, one of the most Christian cities in the civilized world. She persuaded Ethelbert to listen to Augustine, which he did with some misgivings, having heard that Augustine could work magic and was fond of making tails grow on people. This, of course, was an exaggeration, and the upshot of the meeting was that Ethelbert said the monks could teach their religion in his kingdom. He even gave them some houses to live in and teach in. Before long, the king and all the nobles became Christians, and told their serfs and vassals to become Christians too. And that's how England was saved.

No doubt Augustine hoped to be recalled to Corporation headquarters, as it is normal business practice to bring back executives who are successful out in the field and give them a good job at the home office. But Gregory told Augustine to stay in Britain. He did, however, name him bishop, which made him the first bishop of England. Perhaps this mollified Augustine somewhat.

---

[4] The Anglo-Saxons spelled practically all their words with four letters.

HOW TO CONVERT PAGANS AT THE LOWEST POSSIBLE COST

We see another example of Gregory's administrative skill in his correspondence, still extant, with Augustine. Gregory was a prolific giver of good advice on how to be an efficient administrator.

Don't tear down the Anglo-Saxon pagan temples, he wrote to Augustine. Building costs are fierce. Turn the temples into Christian churches. Think of the money this will save!

Don't abolish idol worship right off the bat, he counseled Augustine. The Anglo-Saxons set great store by their idol worship. The smart thing to do is to get them to shift over, a little at a time, from the worship of idols to the worship of Christian saints. After all, there isn't a great deal of difference between the worship of idols and the worship of saints. Pretty soon the English will hardly notice they aren't worshiping their old idols any more.

Here we have perhaps the first recorded example of what is known in modern business parlance as "transference of brand loyalty." It is the strategy of not knocking the competition but working quietly to steal its customers.

Gregory also recommended to Augustine that he not forbid the English their old pagan customs just because they had become Christians. It isn't easy, he wrote, for wicked people to give up their evil ways, but it isn't so hard if they do it a little at a time.

We bring this up because it was this last advice which accounts for our calling Easter Easter in our Western Christian culture today. The English already had Easter before they became Christians, only for them it was the festival of the sun goddess, whose name is Eastre. Augustine just changed the reason for the celebration, but thought it unnecessary to change the name of the occasion. This is why all Christians[5] today call our greatest holy day by the name of the Anglo-Saxon sun goddess.

[5] All English-speaking Christians, that is. Since English-speaking Christians hold that the only authentic version of Holy Writ was dictated by the Almighty in King James English, and since it is in the English-speaking Christian Corporation where the action is today, what other Christians call Easter is of negligible importance.

We know that you have always wondered why Gregory I is called Gregory the Great, and we hope that you can now see why. He is of such paramount importance in the history of the Christian Corporation because (1) by his success he confirmed the Corporation's conviction that if you have to choose, administrative skill is better than piety in Corporation leadership; (2) he illustrated the business wisdom of never standing still but always seeking new markets and expanded territory for the Corporation; and (3) he nailed down England for the Christian Corporation, thus assuring all future English-speaking countries a Christian civilization. Otherwise, you and I might still be chasing each other around trees with stone axes like our Anglo-Saxon forebears.

Oddly enough, the uninformed layman remembers Gregory today because he invented the Gregorian chant, which he didn't. He probably could have invented it, though, if he had wanted to.

IX. *Charlemagne knocks together the Holy Roman Empire*

The world was not at its best when Charlemagne came on the scene. Alcuin of York, who was supposed to be the smartest man alive at the time, described the era as "these loveless days of the world's last age." We now know that his judgment was somewhat premature. We also know that learned men in any era have a weakness for melancholy predictions and pronouncements of imminent doom for the planet. However, we must recognize that Alcuin's gloomy estimate had some basis in fact.

For one thing, the Roman Empire was in a state of near collapse, which meant that the Christian Corporation was in danger of collapse. At one time the empire had ruled Frankland, a very large territory which included parts of what today we call France and Germany. But the legions had been gone for several centuries, and with them had gone the firm control of religious life exercised by the Christian Corporation. The Frankish people, though still nominally Christian, were more noted as barbarians than as Christians. We modern Christians associate the term barbarian with uncouth habits and brutish traits of character. This is not entirely incorrect, but it would be better if we thought of barbarians as just culturally deprived and ethically underdeveloped. You can be a barbarian and a good Christian, as we shall see from the life of Charlemagne.

Let us first get Charlemagne placed in history. His grandfather was Charles Martel, who wasn't a king at all but just an advisor to the Merovingian kings. As you will remember, the Merovingian kings weren't much, and before he died Charles Martel divided their kingdom up among his own sons, one of whom was Pippin the Short. Pippin the Short was Charlemagne's father, so Charlemagne was born a prince.

Charlemagne was a bastard. We mean this not in the sense that the term is applied today as an uncomplimentary judgment on another person's character or personality, but in the technical meaning of the word. We mustn't be upset by this, though, because Pippin was a very Christian king and later on married Charlemagne's mother in a church ceremony with little Prince Charles as an attendant. Barbarians, even Christian barbarians, had not yet learned to be as concerned about the niceties of legitimatizing one's offsprings as we modern middle-class Christians are.

Let us now catch a glimpse of what daily conditions of life were like if you were a barbarian. We will see this through the eyes of Désirée, a princess of the Lombards, whom Charlemagne married when he was quite young. He was already married at the time to a girl named Himiltrud and had a son by her. But these young marriages don't always work out, so he sent Himiltrud back to her father because, of course, bigamy is a sin in the eyes of the Church.[1]

The Lombards, who lived in Italy, were not considered especially refined, and have bequeathed no monuments of consequence to the culture of mankind. In fact, the pope—in a letter to Charlemagne on the occasion of his marriage to Désirée—speaks of the Lombards as "the treacherous and fouly stinking race of Lombards, which is not numbered among the nations except that the tribe of lepers has sprung from it." We would not expect, then, that Désirée's requirements for personal cleanliness and comfort would overtax the facilities of a fourth-rate hotel. But even she was appalled at living conditions in Ingelheim, Charlemagne's capital city.

---

[1] Martin Luther, some 800 years later, said he much preferred bigamy to divorce, but that bigamy was only Christian if you kept it secret. Keeping bigamy a secret is not as easy as it sounds, so Christians—especially kings—usually favor divorce, or annulment as the Church calls it because divorce is, of course, also a sin.

The royal palace, it seems, was separated from the market place only by a wooden wall shored up by dung heaps where the pigs rooted all day. The palace did have some faded Roman paintings of fauns chasing nymphs, which is a nice touch in any home. However, the palace smelled like a cowshed all the time. This was because it was next door to the royal cowshed. Also, the royal Seneschal employed the palace yard for raising chickens, ducks and pheasants, and a yardful of poultry doesn't do much to tone up a place.

The palace roof, Désirée discovered, was given over to the raising of jubarb herbs because jubarb herbs ward off lightning. Jubarb herbs also pep up a pot roast if you don't have any A-1 or Worcestershire sauce handy. The royal gardens were planted with fruit trees wherever there was room between statues of Roman emperors left over from better days. The gardens were swarming with pigeons, and an orchard full of statues with flocks of fruit-filled pigeons overhead isn't the best place to take a walk, so Désirée stayed indoors most of the time.

THE DIETARY AND OTHER HABITS OF A CHRISTIAN KING

Désirée also found her new husband's personal habits somewhat beneath her own modest standards. He wanted roast meat every evening for dinner—he would eat roasted anything. He wanted it brought to him from the spit scorching hot, and then he would stuff it in his mouth with both hands. He slept in his underwear. When he got up at dawn for morning prayers he wrapped some leggings on and donned a smelly old sheepskin bathrobe and went off to church. On the infrequent occasions when he felt the need of a bath he went to a nearby warm mineral spring where everyone in town, including the king, swam in the buff. Désirée had enough of this in a short time, and when she left she was in such a hurry to get out of there that she forgot to take her personal silver dishes with her.

Like Désirée, we are apt to be censorious of such personal crudity. It is hard for us to see how a person can be a Christian and at the same time tolerate body odor. While we would never question the efficacy of mouthwash as an aid to sanctity, nor denigrate the beatitudinous effect of the daily bath, we must bear in mind that these blessings have been bestowed on us by modern technology, and urged on us by modern, middle-class Christian culture. There were no deodorant or talcum powder or hair-stickum ads to inform eighth-century barbarians that personal grooming is a godly trait, so how was Charlemagne to know?

While he may have possessed personal tendencies we find repellent, there is no denying Charlemagne's position of an all-time hero of the Christian Corporation. His main claim to veneration by the Corporation is that he knocked together the Holy Roman Empire.

Charlemagne and his younger brother Carloman had divided Pippin's kingdom. Carloman was more refined than Charlemagne, and Charlemagne claimed that their daddy always liked Carloman best, so the two boys weren't as friendly as they might have been. Carloman died quite young, and when Charlemagne heard of his brother's death he decided it would be fitting for him to attend the funeral. He thoughtfully took with him a regiment or two, and after the obsequies announced that he was king of his brother's territory. Carloman's widow and some local politicians put up a feeble protest that Carloman's sons were the rightful heirs to the kingdom, but a regiment of soldiers is always a stronger argument than mere hereditary rights, as many an Arab who formerly resided in Jerusalem will tell you, so Charlemagne's argument won. This was really the beginning of the Holy Roman Empire, although no one knew it at the time.

In those primitive times there was simply no way to found the Holy Roman Empire and thus strengthen the Christian Corporation except by warfare, because the various nations and races did not understand as well as they should have the benefits, both temporal and spiritual, which would accrue to them as members of the empire.

CHARLEMAGNE THE CHRISTIAN WARRIOR

It was as a fearsome Christian warrior that Charlemagne first made his mark on history, and is, as a matter of fact, how we think of him today. Napoleon considered Charlemagne one of history's military geniuses, but recent research inclines as to the view that it was sometimes more luck than genius which accounted for his success.

For one thing, the Franks were not ideal soldiers. Charlemagne had about three or four thousand horsemen,[2] but they couldn't ride very well and kept falling off their horses. They were equipped with lances and haubergeons,[3] and with two swords—a long one for slashing and a short one for ripping. There were also three or four thousand foot soldiers, less impressively equipped, tagging along.

We are told that the horsemen presented an awesome sight as they charged the enemy. The signal to charge was given by blowing a lot of trumpets, very loud. Trumpets affected Franks much as bagpipes affect Scots, so they would get all excited and gallop forward screaming and yelling and swearing too. This should have disconcerted any enemy, no matter how brave, except that experience had taught most of their enemies that as soon as the Franks got close enough to the opposition to do any actual fighting, the Franks lost their enthusiasm rather quickly and charged right back to where they had started from.

One important step in the founding of the Holy Roman Empire came about when the pope sent Charlemagne a message that the Lombards were about to capture Rome and would Charlemagne hurry down and deliver him? A more prudent king, whose army was as defective as Charlemagne's, would have declined the honor of defending the Vatican. But Charlemagne was a stout Christian

[2] The Franks had a superstitious prejudice against being numbered exactly, so the figure on just how many soldiers Charlemagne had are about as reliable as Premier Castro's estimate of the Cuban sugar cane harvest.
[3] I don't know what they are either.

and felt that he had to answer the summons from the chairman of the Christian Corporation.

It isn't an easy trip from Frankland to Italy because you have to go over the Alps. Soldiers sometimes get tired and dispirited doing nothing but climbing over mountains, so Charlemagne had them sing hymns as they marched. One of the hymns said

> Turn your heads and look again
> This road will bring us back
>   to the Fatherland.

which may not have won the Nobel prize for poetry, but is certainly no worse than many of the hymns we sing today, and is better than some.

When they got to where the Lombards were camped, Charlemagne offered to bribe the enemy. He said he would give them fourteen thousand pieces of silver if they would just go away, but they wouldn't. So everybody sat around for a month or so trying to figure out what to do. Finally, some of Charlemagne's officers devised a battle plan which looked promising, and Charlemagne gave the order to charge. When the Lombards saw the Franks coming they ran away as fast as they could, although not before the Franks got a few good cuts at them, and it was a great military victory for the Franks.

Charlemagne was bedazzled by Rome, as country boys always are overwhelmed by their first glimpse of Broadway. In Charlemagne's case it was the myriads of churches with their magnificent forests of columns and thousands of flickering candles that turned him on. He also went dippy over the chanting of the monks at the services, and took a chanting monk home with him to teach his own clergy how to do it and thus add some class to religious rites in Frankland.

We mustn't lead you to believe that Charlemagne was a fierce, warlike, one-dimensional personality, though. He was a many-sided man, one side of which was a sense of Christian charity amazing for the times. He demonstrated this charity on his way home from Rome. All the Lombard leaders had expected that Charlemagne would hang them or worse, as that was the traditional way to treat a conquered enemy. But he didn't. He didn't execute one Lombard, and even more astounding, he didn't exact a penny of tax or tribute from the Lombards, which was as unheard of then as it is today. All he did was to stop by and tell the Lombards that he was now king of Lombardy. Then he went on back to Frankland so he could get the hay mowing done before bad weather.

But, as people frequently feel about people who have done them a big favor, the Lombards hated Charlemagne for his benevolence toward them. He was no sooner out of sight than they started plotting against him and revolting and saying Charlemagne wasn't king of them at all. So Charlemagne had to turn around and come back and do it all over again. This time he hung a lot of Lombards, and then the Lombards understood that though Charlemagne was full of Christian compassion he wasn't a sissy, and that it would be better for them not to fool around with him any more but do what he said.

The significance of the conquering of the Lombards is that it teaches us that Christian firmness works better than Christian charity when dealing with Lombards. Also, the victory over the Lombards was a large step toward the founding of the Holy Roman Empire.

THE DIFFICULT CONVERSION OF THE HEATHEN SAXONS

The Saxons, who lived not in Saxony as we would expect, but in Hanover, Brunswick, Oldenburg, and Westphalia as they are known today, were next door neighbors to the Franks, but not very good ones. There could have been no true and lasting Holy Roman Empire without subjugating the Saxons, and Charlemagne undertook the task, but it wasn't easy.

Saxons are worse than barbarians, because barbarians—Frankish barbarians anyway—are Christians, whereas Saxons are heathens. The Saxons had kooky religious ideas such as worshiping a couple of trees—one named Yggdrasill, which was a big ash and was supposed to hold up the world according to Saxon theology, and one named Irminsul which was sort of a surrogate for Yggdrasill when it was inconvenient to worship Yggdrasill.[4] As you can readily see, people who harbor such outrageous theological concepts, and indulge in heathenish rites and rituals, and expected their gods would do all kinds of good things for them if they only went through the right pious motions, would be an offense to any upstanding Christians in the neighborhood. They were an offense to Charlemagne, and he knew he had to do something about them.

Now we must keep in mind that Charlemagne, unlike many Christian kings who were only nominal Christians because it was better politics for them to be Christian than something else, was the real goods. He bore the title *Christianissimus Rex,* which was awarded only to the genuine article. And if we need more evidence of his piety we only need to recall that when he was in Rome he spent most of his time discussing church discipline with the pope. You have to be a pretty good Christian to find the subject of church discipline all that fascinating.[5]

It was, then, primarily from missionary zeal, that Charlemagne decided to do something about the Saxons. Some missionary priests were accordingly sent into Saxon land. But the Saxons had an annoying habit of killing Christian missionaries, which in turn irritated Charlemagne. So, according to reliable sources, Charlemagne said that he was going to "attack the perfidious and truce-breaking nation of the Saxons in war, and persevere therein until they were either conquered and made subject to the Christian religion or were altogether swept off the face of the earth."

This probably isn't exactly what Charlemagne said. It sounds to us like a cleaned-up version of what a barbarian Christian king would say when he was real sore at somebody. It is likely to be what the royal phrasemaker said Charlemagne said. However he said it, what

---

[4] Some authorities say Irminsul was not a tree but a big wooden column. However, we are unable to verify this, so let's just say it was a sacred tree, but not as sacred as Yggdrasill.

[5] Pope Hadrian I, with whom Charlemagne carried on these conversations, was even more fascinated by the subject of church discipline than Charlemagne. In his twenty-four years as pope he convened thirty-three ecclesiastical councils, mostly for the purpose of discussing church discipline. Any modern church or denomination would convene vastly more than thirty-three ecclesiastical councils in any twenty-four-year period, of course, but not just for the purpose of discussing church discipline.

Charlemagne meant was that the Saxons would accept Christianity or else.

The missionary strategy of offering heathens the choice of conversion or death is nearly always cheaper and more efficient than sending priests, so long as you have a big enough army. Charlemagne did have a big enough army. There was a little trouble at first because some of the Saxons were reluctant to give up their heathenish absurdities. But after he killed a batch of them the word got around, and pretty soon multitudes of Saxons were flocking in from every glade and forest and requesting baptism.

Public sentiment would prohibit us from evangelizing this way today, because today the only acceptable war is one we start for political reasons. But there is no getting around the fact that Charlemagne's way is the fastest, surest, and maybe the cheapest way of winning converts ever devised.[6]

After his tremendous success in converting the Saxons, Charlemagne went off to invade Spain and convert the Mohammedan Moors who were as thick as fleas on a dog in Spain. The Spanish campaign was not a success, because the Moors lived in walled cities and declined to come outside and fight. Since Charlemagne didn't have any tanks or anything to knock the walls down, he finally had to abandon the Moors to their iniquitous religious practices and go back to Frank land.

But in his absence, some of the Saxons who evidently hadn't been converted to Christianity as soundly as they might have been, invaded Frank land and burned and raped and pillaged and killed some of the priests who had baptized them. It is undeniable that the Saxons' conduct was not markedly different from that of the Christian Franks when they invaded the Saxons. But we must not forget that the Franks did what they did for good Christian reasons, and the Saxons did what they did for bad heathen reasons, and this makes all the difference, because Christian moral theologians constantly assure us that it is the intent of a deed and not the deed itself which determines its moral and

[6] It is still acceptable, of course, in fact almost mandatory, to inject massive doses of religion into wars we start for political reasons. This is because people feel much better about killing other people if they can sing "Praise the Lord and Pass the Ammunition" while they are doing it.

ethical purity. If any of our more squeamish readers find this hard to stomach, pretend that the Franks were Americans and the Saxons were Communists. All of us know that it is very wicked and unchristian for Communists to kill Americans, but that it is very righteous and godly for Americans to kill Communists. When you look at it this way it should clear up the problem for you.

Charlemagne, of course, could not tolerate such behavior on the part of the Saxons. So he had another Saxon campaign in which he subjugated the Saxons again. Then, when the Franks left, the Saxons abandoned Christianity again. For several years running Charlemagne would have, each year, a Saxon campaign in which the Saxons would get converted to Christianity, then, as soon as the Franks left, they would revert to their disgusting pagan practices.

THE CAPITULATIO DE PARTIBUS SAXONIAE

When it became evident that converting Saxons was a tiresome business, Charlemagne marched an army into Saxon land and promulgated the *Capitulatio de Partibus Saxoniae,* which means "If you heathens go on resisting our efforts to convert you, here is what is going to happen to you." Some of the rules laid down in the *Capitulatio* were:

(1) No one is to rob a church—penalty: death.
(2) Failure to observe Lent (such as eating a steak during the forty days)—penalty: hanging.[7]
(3) For the practice of witchcraft—penalty: death.
(4) For practicing cremation instead of burial—penalty: death.
(5) For any Saxon who goes off and hides in order to escape being baptized—penalty: death. (You could escape execution, though, if you went to a priest and confessed and did penance and promised to be a good Christian from then on.)

[7] There was a rider on this rule which said that you wouldn't be hung if a priest certified that you needed to eat meat for the good of your health. Many people who were partial to steaks and roasts even during Lent thought it a good idea to cultivate a priest.

The part of the new law the priests liked best was the part that said everyone had to tithe. In case you don't understand the law about tithing, the Old Testament required that all Hebrews give one tenth of their annual adjusted gross income to the Temple. The New Testament doesn't have this requirement, but Christians just assumed that it held over from the Old Testament and was binding on them too—or at least this is how the clergy interpreted it. However, not all Christians are as generous with the Church when the tithe is a custom as they are when the tithe is a law. When it has a choice, the Church always prefers that tithing be a law instead of just voluntary.[8] So Charlemagne passed a law which said, "We enact that according to the command of God, all men, whether nobles, freeborn men, or *liti* (serfs), shall give the tenth part of their substance and labour to the churches and priests." As you can see, this took in everyone (except priests). Charlemagne didn't fool around with oil depletion allowances or tax-free municipals.

The Saxons didn't care much for these new laws. They started another revolt, and managed to slaughter quite a few Franks. Then Charlemagne, no doubt remembering how he had had to deal with the recalcitrant Lombards, rounded up forty-five hundred Saxons who were identifiable as leaders of the revolt and instead of reading the riot act to them as he usually did, he butchered the whole lot. Lopping off forty-five hundred heads is a grueling amount of labor and well-nigh exhausted the executioners and the burial detail. Charlemagne's forthright strategy helped a lot, but it was another twenty years before the Saxons became docile Christians and Saxon land a part of the Holy Roman Empire.

CHARLEMAGNE—A NUT ABOUT EDUCATION

We are pleased to report that fighting valorously to convert pagans and knock together the Holy Roman Empire is not Charle-

---

[8] The modern church feels the same way about this as the Church has always felt. If you don't believe it, just listen to the howls of anguish arising from all the ecclesiastical headquarters when some tax reformer proposes to knock out the charitable deduction clause of the tax law.

magne's only bequest to the glories of the Christian Corporation. He was equally bold in his espousal of education as a duty of a Christian king, although his military exploits overshadow his scholarly triumphs, because warriors generally receive a better press than scholars.

Although he couldn't read or write, Charlemagne was nutty about education. In those days a Christian king who knew how to fight, and settle disputes, and hold his hooch with the best drinking men in the kingdom, was considered an adequate Christian king. But Charlemagne was not content with these modest accomplishments. He wanted to educate himself and educate his people.

As a start on a program of national education he imported Alcuin of York, whom we mentioned earlier as being the most learned man in the world at the time, as secretary for education and culture, although that wasn't his title. Alcuin wrote poetry, and wondered about such things as how a nightingale could be so small and make such big, beautiful music. He took long walks through pastures without playing golf or hunting rabbits or pheasants. He was a bachelor. Today we would look on Alcuin as an effete intellectual snob whose opinions carry no weight in the society of hardheaded, practical, down-to-earth men, who are the true backbone and fountain of wisdom of our society. But Charlemagne, who was never accused of being an effete intellectual snob, curiously didn't feel this way about Alcuin. He loved to have him around. He used Alcuin as a sort of portable encyclopedia or reference library.

We could wish that Charlemagne had stressed solid vocational training in his educational programs, because everyone respects vocational training. But Charlemagne had an unfortunate weakness for what we now call the humanities, meaning poetry and philosophy and the arts and other nice and decorative but useless subjects that are today relegated to musty and obscure corners of our great universities.

Charlemagne, for example, might well have wanted an educational program in pig raising or hop growing or barrelmaking. These subjects would seem appropriate to us. But what he wanted was for the Franks to be tutored in the use of Latin. He thought the Franks would pray better prayers if they learned to pray in Latin. It wasn't that he believed God failed to understand the Rhineland dialects in which the Franks normally prayed. Nor did he believe that God was a snob and would only pay attention to prayers in an elegant language long associated with pious and ecclesiastical utterances. Charlemagne was a practical man and he had a practical reason for his preference for prayers in Latin. He knew that his people were wont to let their minds wander during prayers. What most of them were thinking while praying, he suspected, was about fornication, drinking, ways of loafing on the job, brawling, and other agreeable forms of passing the time. Charlemagne suspected this was what they thought about during prayers because it was what he thought about during prayers. But he had discovered, since learning a little Latin himself, that it was more difficult to think crude and lewd thoughts in Latin than it was to think them in one's native tongue. Thus his national Latin project.

Eventually the national education program included grammar, dialectics, rhetoric, mathematics, algebra, music, medicine and astronomy. There were no teachers at all to be had in Frank land, so Charlemagne imported teachers from England and Lombardy. There must have been an educational establishment of some kind in Frank land, though, because there was an outcry that Charlemagne was favoring foreigners and intellectualism, which is how any modern teachers union would react if President Nixon started importing teachers from England and Lombardy, which we are sure he won't. But kings do not operate under the same handicaps that presidents suffer. Kings can do anything they damn please, so Charlemagne went right on with his educational program.

One unanticipated spin-off from the educational venture was the development of a fast, efficient national news service. Educators in any age like to keep in touch with one another. Today they do this through frequent professional conferences in Atlantic City and San Francisco and other exotic places. Back then, though, travel was not so simple and you couldn't get a jet ticket to Hawaii just by presenting an expense voucher, so Alcuin and his fellow scholars had to make do with correspondence. Alcuin had scholarly buddies everywhere, and pretty soon Charlemagne caught on that he was a goldmine of current political information and palace gossip.

On top of this, at about the same time the principle of the carrier pigeon was discovered, or at least discovered by Charlemagne. This enabled a message to be sent from, say, Rome to Ingelheim in a shorter elapsed time than it would take today despite our jet planes and the bureaucratic efficiency of our post offices.

THE REFORM OF THE CLERGY—A DIFFICULT UNDERTAKING

Another spin-off of the education project was a program to reform the clergy, an unpromising enterprise in any age. It came about when Charlemagne tried to enlist the clergy in the services of the education project. He instructed his priests to preach about glories of the mind only to discover that most of the priests not only never preached at all but didn't have a clue as to how to go about preparing or delivering a sermon.

The clerical reform act forbade the abbots and abbesses to own hunting dogs or falcons, and said they shouldn't carry on love affairs or enter into profit-making ventures, which gives us an idea of how the eighth-century Christian clergy passed the days and nights.

Another item in the reform bill was that the clergy had to preach at services instead of just mumbling the Mass, which was the custom. We don't know that there was any great demand for sermons on the part of the parishioners, but Charlemagne thought there should be preaching, and what he thought counted most.

In order to demonstrate to the clergy how to preach a good sermon, Charlemagne—who, so far as we know, never attended theological seminary or passed a course in homiletics—went on a preaching mission himself, an enterprise not commonly undertaken by kings. If we can believe the reports he was one heck of a fine preacher. Even discounting the normally good press accorded kings and Billy Graham and such people, he must have been pretty good.

Now we come to one of the banner days, one of the great dates in the saga of the Christian Corporation. It happened on Christmas day of the year 800, a convenient date to remember. By this date Charlemagne, through luck or genius, was ruler of all of the territory now known as France, Belgium and Holland. He controlled about half of Germany as well as Austria-Hungary, some of Spain, and a good 50 per cent of Italy.

CHRISTMAS DAY A.D. 800—A GREAT DATE FOR THE CHRISTIAN CORPORATION

On Christmas day, A.D. 800, Charlemagne was in Rome. He attended early Mass at St. Peter's. The records are rather spotty as to exactly what happened, but historians claim that the pope, whose name was Leo III, had persuaded Charlemagne to come to church dressed as a noble Roman. To dress as a noble Roman you have to put on a sort of nightgown and wear dainty slippers. Knowing Charlemagne as we do, this seems about as likely as John Wayne going out to dinner wearing hippie beads and carrying a purse. Nightgown or no nightgown, when Charlemagne stood up after saying his prayers, the pope slipped up behind him and placed a crown on his head. Then the congregation shouted, "To Charles, Augustus, crowned by God, great and peace-giving Emperor—long life and victory!" Since shouts like this seldom get shouted without several rehearsals, we conclude that Leo had been planning this little drama for some time, especially as the people repeated the shout, word-for-word and in unison, not once but twice. Then Leo draped a royal-purple cloak around Charlemagne's shoulders and in the Mass referred to him as "Imperator." This meant that he was now officially the Holy Roman Emperor.

THE HOLY ROMAN EMPIRE EXPLAINED

In these sad, secularized days when the pope no longer creates emperors but has a hard time holding his own clergy in line, it is not easy to explain the concept of the Holy Roman Empire, but we will try.

Perhaps the best way to put it is that a visible Holy Roman Empire underlines the idea that the secular corporation, or the State, and the Christian Corporation, or the Church, are but the two faces of the same entity, or at least a very close partnership. The State, men wanted to believe, existed to aid them in the achievement of temporal happiness. The Church had the more important task of leading men to eternal bliss. This explanation takes care of the holy and the empire parts. The Roman part had to do with men's belief that in Charlemagne and his conquests they saw a recrudescence of the old Roman Empire which had flourished and ruled so beneficently in times past, but by the eighth century had fallen into decay. Charlemagne, historians tell us, was—more than any other king or emperor or sovereign in history—headman over all things in his own time.

It is true, of course, that when Charlemagne died fourteen years later[9] the Holy Roman Empire began to come apart at the seams. One cause of the decline was that Charlemagne's son and heir, Louis the Pious, spent too much time praying and not enough fighting. Here we have ample evidence that to be a successful Holy Roman Emperor you not only need to be holy, but you had better be a tough baby as well.[10]

As we look upon the life and works of Carolus Magnus, or Charlemagne, we are moved to awe and wonder. It is true that modern, refined Christians feel that Charlemagne's table manners

[9] He died from catching a bad cold while out hunting, which is an inglorious exit for a Holy Roman Emperor. He was seventy-two years old at the time and should have known better.

[10] As a matter of fact, Louis' three sons took the empire away from him and divided it up among themselves. Their names were Lothair, Charles the Bald, and Louis the German. None of them was anything like as pious as their old man.

and lack of sexual inhibitions are offensive, and perhaps not entirely Christian. He comes in for some little criticism of his forthright methods of evangelizing the heathen Saxons. And, on occasion, he may have been overly firm with the Lombards. However, if history teaches us anything it is that Christian kings require more latitude for their personal habits and political action than mere civilian Christians.

The world isn't nearly so full as it once was of kings, and the ethical philosophy that it is permissible for some Christians, namely kings, to be less than circumspect in their personal behavior has been democratized and made available to everyone. Today we call this ethical philosophy "the new morality."

On the other hand, Charlemagne had many splendid attributes. He was sincerely pious. He was a fearsome military leader. He was zealous to build up and increase the holdings of the Christian Corporation. These are all characteristics which the Christian Corporation values in kings.

On top of this, he was just, and sometimes merciful to a fault. He was a patron of education and the arts. Taking into account the lower standards of everything prevailing in the eighth century, especially among barbarians, we have to rate him quite high as kings go, although this is not an exacting standard.

These laudable traits which he exhibited are just as irrelevant, though, as his less endearing habits. From the point of view of the health and prosperity of the Christian Corporation, which is the point of view we espouse, the only item that counts is what did he do for the Corporation.

What he did was to fix firmly in the minds and affections of mankind the vision of the political corporation and the Christian Corporation marching down through history hand in hand. He was the first genuine Holy Roman Emperor, and in our estimate you just can't do much better than that.

X. *The ninth century—theology prospers, and the Pope firms up his position with the pseudo-Isidorian decretals*

Some historians claim that the ninth century, after the death of Charlemagne, was a dismal chapter in the annals of mankind, but we think we can demonstrate that it was one of the best centuries ever.

For one thing, the ninth century was a time of intellectual triumphs dazzling to behold. John Scotus Erigena, scholar to the court of Charles the Bald, translated the *Pseudo-Dionysius,* a task long neglected.[1] He also developed a new brand of Neo-Platonic philosophy. We now know that this philosophy was heretical, but they didn't know it back then, so we presume it did them no lasting harm.

THE THEOLOGICAL POT BOILS

It was also in the ninth century that a French monk named Paschasius Radbertus wrote the first thoroughgoing treatise on the Lord's Supper, and none too soon we think. In his treatise Radbertus agreed with Augustine, or Latin theology, that the elements of the supper—bread and wine—become Christ's body to those

[1] This work, best described as the first, definitive treatment on angels, was supposed to have been written by Dionysius the Areopagite in the fifth century. We are indebted to it for the information that among angelic beings the Archangel Michael is most honored.

who partake in faith. He also agreed with the Greeks that by divine miracle the elements become the actual flesh and blood of Christ. It occurs to us that these two views are not entirely reconcilable, but ninth-century Christians apprehended no discrepancies here, so we shouldn't worry ourselves about it.

Other intellectual ferment during the ninth century was brewed by Hrabanus Maurus and a monk named Ratramnus. They got a lot of public visibility by attacking the doctrines of Radbertus, saying No, the elements didn't change during the Mass and were afterward the same old bread and wine they were before consecration. It would gratify us to read that the authorities cracked down on Maurus and Ratramnus, but they didn't.

Then there was Gottschalk of Fulda, who came out strongly for double divine predestination, a wholesome and helpful doctrine strongly recommended by Augustine of Hippo several centuries earlier. It puzzles us, therefore, as to why the authorities accused Gottschalk of heresy and put him in jail for twenty years when all he had done was to borrow some dogma from Augustine, the soundest of orthodox theologians. All we can surmise is that navigating the streams of orthodox theology was tricky business in the ninth century, just as it is today. Today, though, you are more likely to go to jail, or at least lose your job, for expounding heretical political theology.

So you can see that the ninth century was a time of prosperity for theology, and much intellectual progress was made. But more significant still, it was a time when the position of pope as head of the Christian Corporation was firmed up. More than this, papal control over political and secular affairs was extended, which was beneficial to everyone.

THE HOLY INSIGHT OF NICHOLAS I

These great strides forward were accomplished largely by Pope Nicholas I. With the holy insight given to popes he perceived Corporation who would also be able to dictate to princes and kings that what the world needed was a strong head of the Christian and other political rulers. People with overdeveloped predilections for democratic forms of government find such an idea repugnant, but they just don't understand conditions in the ninth century. Charles the Bald was Holy Roman Emperor, but not a very good one, and all the kings and other rulers did about as they pleased. The situation was similar to what things would be like if President Nixon let Lester Maddox be Prince of Georgia, and George Wallace be king of four or five southern states, and Ronald Reagan be Count of California, and Mayor Daley be Duke of Chicago, which of course he already is. We can readily see that such a situation would be intolerable, and Pope Nicholas I found political conditions in the ninth century intolerable.

However, not everyone in the ninth century was prepared to admit that the pope merited such power. It was not that they didn't like Nicholas I, who was probably a pleasant enough fellow, at least as likable and charming as Senator Stennis or Attorney General Mitchell. What people said was that there was no tradition by which the pope could be recognized as head of practically everything. In the ninth century, tradition counted for much more than it does today except with the Daughters of the American Revolution and the older Yale alumni.

PROVIDENCE PROVIDES THE DECRETALS

This crisis might have gone unresolved, with consequences too fearful to imagine, had it not been that at this time the pseudo-Isidorian decretals were discovered. We can account for this fortuitous discovery only on the theory that it was the intervention of divine providence, and you will see why when we tell you about it.

The word "decretals" sounds like the name of a flower, but decretals are collections of the decrees of popes. The pseudo-Isidorian decretals was epic in dimension, containing all the significant decisions of every pope from Clement in the first century, before the concept of pope had been born, to Gregory II in the eighth century. It was the work of Isidore of Seville, a learned

Spanish bishop who was made saint later on. How Isidore, who died sometime around 636, could have authored a document which included popes in the eighth century is a question which troubles us a little, but it in no way diminished the authenticity of the decretals in the eyes of the ninth-century faithful, so we shouldn't worry about it. Probably the people of the ninth century looked upon the pseudo-Isidorian decretals much as we look on the stories of George Washington never telling a lie and throwing a dollar across the Potomac. When you examine the stories too carefully certain discrepancies can be noted, but we know they are true stories for all that, so the discrepancies really don't hurt at all.

The important point for us to remember about the pseudo-Isidorian decretals is that, by reference to it, everyone could read that all the popes over eight centuries of church history had concurred in the conviction that the pope has supreme authority over practically everything. We cannot understand why historians want to be picky and say that these decretals were spurious and call them pseudo, which means fake. After all, they surely do not misrepresent the views of the pontiffs. The claim that you are head of everything, which some people find a trifle excessive, no doubt seems a modest and reasonable claim if you happen to be pope. Anyway, everybody said, Yes, we can see by the Isidorian decretals that the pope is unquestionably the supreme authority, and we surely need one with the mess we are in.

Nicholas I, though he agreed completely with the tradition established by the discovery of the pseudo-Isidorian decretals, and even advanced some claims for the authority of the bishop of Rome which made the claims of the decretals seem somewhat diffident, knew that it takes more than talk and tradition to establish your authority.[2] So Nicholas slapped down an archbishop, Hincmar of Rheims by name, for some petty reason or maybe no reason at all, which was a way of showing the clergy that the

---

[2] Modern popes understand this just as well as Nicholas did. Pope Paul, for example, speaks frequently about the tradition of his office. He intersperses the speeches, though, with decrees such as banning the pill and ordering the clergy to lay off discussing priestly celibacy. He knows that he has to crack down now and then to show who is boss or pretty soon people would quit doing what he tells them to do.

pope was the supreme authority over the clergy.[3] Then, to show that he was the supreme authority over kings, he slapped down King Lothaire II of Lorraine. What happened was that Lothaire had divorced his wife Thietberga to marry his concubine Waldrada. Nicholas undivorced him, which was most embarrassing to Lothaire, although it is unlikely that he radically altered his living arrangements.

NICHOLAS OPPOSES MICHAEL THE DRUNKARD

Pursuing his pious purpose of establishing the power of the pontiff by decisive action, Nicholas went looking for bigger game. He took on Michael the Drunkard, Christian Emperor of Constantinople. Nicholas said Michael was failing to observe some item of ecclesiastical discipline. The issue was no doubt of pristine relevance at the time, but the exact nature of the controversy, we regret to relate, has disappeared in the miasma of ecclesiastical history and we are unable to fish it out. Michael the Drunkard didn't take kindly to Nicholas I trying to push him around, though, and responded by calling Nicholas and all Roman Christians heretics. We would look on such a charge as laughable, except that Michael pointed out that Roman Christians fasted on Saturday, and also they ate milk, butter and cheese during Lent, which is heresy indeed.

In spite of this setback by Michael the Drunkard we mustn't minimize the contribution of Nicholas I to the health and well-being of the Christian Corporation. Standing on the rock of tradition provided him in so timely a manner by the discovery of the pseudo-Isidorian decretals, he proceeded to push people around until everybody had it firmly fixed in their thinking that the chairman of the Christian Corporation is supposed to push people around. His bold and holy administration unified the Corporation, scared the dickens out of potential heretics, and made it a lot

[3] We do not need to feel sorry for Hincmar, however. He was an old tyrant, very dictatorial with the people under him, a veritable autocrat. We, as well as Nicholas I, look on these qualities not only as unchristian but downright offensive.

easier for future popes to exercise the prerogatives of divinely granted power. Countless leaders have been accounted rousing successes on lesser credentials than these. Anyone who would expect more than this as one man's contribution to history, the welfare of the Christian Corporation, and the good of mankind would be unreasonable indeed.

XI. *The great picture controversy divides the Christian Corporation*

Up to now our story of the Christian Corporation has been a tale of heartening success, with, of course, occasional difficulties here and there such as beset any aggressive business enterprise. In the eleventh century, though, the Corporation suffered a serious setback, a blow comparable in magnitude to that suffered by Standard Oil when the government split up the one gigantic corporation into smaller competing companies. This was the great division of 1054 when the Christian Corporation divided into the Roman, or Western, or Catholic Corporation, and the Orthodox, or Eastern Corporation.

Before we tell you about it, let us remind you that this wasn't the first time the Corporation had been riven by controversy and defiled by heresy. The first Christian heresy, or split-off, was something called Gnosticism. You don't need to know anything about Gnosticism except that it challenged the young, shaky Pearly Gates Syndicate back in the second century. Gnosticism wanted to peddle a new brand of salvation. It said you do not get your ticket to heaven by belonging to a salvation syndicate. You get it by gnosis, which means knowledge.

At first glance this appeals to us as a reasonable point of view. Most of us have been taught we are saved by education, learning how to survive in a competitive society, mastering the science of making money in the stock market, things like that. The Gnostics, however, didn't mean this kind of knowledge. They said the knowledge that will save you is the employment of the intellect to achieve identification with pure spirit, a fruitless activity if we ever heard of one.

HOW GNOSTICS GET TO HEAVEN

We wouldn't want you to think that Gnosticism had no attractive features at all. The Gnostics said that only those filled with pure gnosis would be admitted to the best heaven, which they called Pleroma. Since most of us would never even aspire to pure gnosis, this doctrine is rather discouraging, as the Gnostics insisted that anyone without gnosis would inevitably go to the bad place. However, they said, even if you are somewhat in thrall to the evil material world but are not entirely devoid of gnosis, then you will be assigned to a second-grade heaven. This is very much like first class and tourist class on a plane or a boat. First class is much to be preferred over tourist class, but tourist class is better than not going at all. Since nearly everyone thinks he has a little gnosis, we can see why Gnosticism stole a lot of customers from the Christian Corporation, which was a lot more particular about who it let into heaven than the Gnostics were.

Gnosticism was vanquished, though not without a struggle. Also vanquished was the Ebionitic schism, which said you couldn't be a Christian without excluding from Christianity everything non-Jewish, as was the Marcionitic[1] schism which said you couldn't be a Christian without excluding from Christianity everything Jewish. Then there was Montanism, and Manichaeism, and Novatianism, and Monophysiteism, not to mention Arianism, Paulicianism, Keltic Christianity, and a whole bagful more.

---

[1] This schism was started by Marcion, a wealthy shipowner who, when he joined the Church, put ten thousand dollars in the collection plate the very first Sunday. He insisted that a Christian must never eat meat or indulge in sexual intercourse. Many Christians, though, wanted to eat meat and indulge in sexual intercourse, so the Church had to excommunicate Marcion, something it seldom does to a member who can drop ten grand in the basket of a Sunday morning. Marcion then started his own church and edited out of the Bible everything he didn't like, so he probably deserves credit for inventing the idea of Christian censorship.

These schisms were minor nuisances, really—no more trouble-some to the Christian Corporation than an occasional spasm of reform movements are troublesome to the Democratic party organization of Jersey City. However, the Corporation decided that if it was going to be pestered from time to time by heretical groups it had better institute a loyalty oath to help people adhere to the true faith. All you had to do to be a Christian, up to this time, was to be baptized and say "Jesus is Lord." We have no criticism of this formula, but it is shockingly inadequate from the organizational point of view. So the Church changed it to saying you accept the official creed of the Church and that you acknowledge the authority of bishops.[2]

UPGRADING THE OFFICE OF BISHOP

We are inclined to look on this step as a giant stride forward, especially the part about acknowledging the authority of bishops. By having bishops, and everyone doing what they say, you have the beginnings of a hierarchy. A hierarchy, as any business education major will tell you, is one of the infallible marks of a true corporation.

However, it was the creation of a hierarchy which issued in the great East-West split of the Christian Corporation. As we have noted previously, in the natural business development of the Christian Corporation the bishop of Rome came to be looked on as chairman of the board.[3] The bishops of Rome never did anything to discourage the idea that the bishop of Rome is number 1, but the bishops of Constantinople were somewhat less enthusiastic about Rome's primacy.

Over the years, we regret to tell you, many differences developed

[2] We are glad to see that Pope Paul, evidently a man who knows his church history, has revived the loyalty oath as an instrument to combat modern schismatics. From now on, Pope Paul has ordered, every R.C. priest must swear his loyalty to his bishop and all that every Maundy Thursday. No doubt this will soon be extended to the R.C. laity, too.

[3] "First among equals" is the way that bishops of Rome like to describe themselves, but everyone knows this is just a kind, Christian way of saying they are boss.

between the part of the Christian Corporation under the supervision of the bishop of Constantinople and the part under the bishop of Rome.

We told you in the last chapter about how the Constantinople or Eastern division of the Corporation was offended by the Roman or Western division's practice of fasting on Saturday and using dairy products during Lent. While all of us find these practices odious as well as a threat to the purity of the faith, we would not deem them sufficient to split the Corporation, and they weren't. There were many other differences which exacerbated the situation also.

Examples of these differences would be the rule in Constantinople that you would be put to death if you didn't believe in the doctrine of the Holy Trinity. Also, since heretical sects had a habit of rebaptizing their converts, Constantinople had a rule that you would be put to death if you allowed yourself to be baptized a second time. Rome, which no doubt was much too lax and permissive with its members, had no such rules. (Although somewhat later Rome did have to adopt the penalty of death for a second dousing in order to deal with the Baptist heresy). We can sympathize, then, with Constantinople's feeling that Roman Christianity wasn't a very serious brand of Christianity since it treated the sin of disbelieving in the Holy Trinity and the sin of rebaptism so lightly.

However, the altercation which issued in the ultimate partition of the Corporation was of a much more serious nature than contentions over the Trinity, baptism, or hierarchical precedence. It is known in ecclesiastical history as the great picture controversy. And while we deplore the division of the Corporation we are glad it was over an issue of genuine importance.

HOW THE PICTURE CONTROVERSY GOT STARTED

The great picture controversy got started during the dark ages. We must keep this in mind, because communications media back then were quite similar to how it is today, even if they didn't have television or the movies. If you wanted to tell a story back then you did it just like you do today—you put together a series of pictures, scenes, statues, whatever, which suggested what you wanted to say. Today we flash these more-or-less connected mosaics on a TV or movie screen. Back then, they put them in the churches. In the Dark Ages, churches were full of this bric-a-brac. Going to church back then was not too different from watching "Laugh-In" today, only the pictures didn't move, and what you saw was a lot of saints and scenes depicting biblical stories instead of Goldie Hawn and Artie Johnson. Although the Dark Ages was somewhat before Marshall McLuhan, they understood full well that the medium is the message.

These pictures were called "icons," which is the Greek word for "image." People became terribly attached to their icons, much as a modern matron will cherish a signed photo of Jimmy Stewart, or younger people will claw and gouge each other to obtain a shred of clothing or a bar of soap used by one of the Beatles.

Most everyone had a personal icon by which they set great store. For example, they would drop their icon down a dry well (after first kissing it, because it didn't work if you didn't kiss it first) and it would bring water back to the well. Naturally we modern Christians find this crudely superstitious and repugnant. We know that novenas, pilgrimages to Lourdes or Fatima, St. Christopher medals,[4] and reading the works of Norman Vincent Peale are much more effective than old-fashioned icons—but we must remember that this was the Dark Ages and there was a lot of superstition mixed in with Christianity back then.

LEO THE ISAURIAN ATTACKS AN ICON

We will relate one incident to show you how attached people were to their icons in those olden days. The emperor of Constantinople, Leo the Isaurian, thought icon worship was getting out of hand, so he ordered some of his soldiers to hack down a big icon

[4] It is true that the Vatican has demoted St. Christopher, but there is as yet no proof whatever that this has in any way mitigated the efficacy of a St. Christopher medal.

which was affixed to the top of the main gate to the city. We would gather that Leo was an intellectual, because intellectuals habitually underestimate the fury of the multitude when denied its popular idols.[5] Anyway, the reaction was comparable to what would happen if the networks canceled "Hee-Haw" or "The Lucy Show." When the soldiers climbed up a ladder to hack down the icon, a mob of pious Christian women pulled the ladders out from under the soldiers, who fell and broke their necks. Then all the pious Christian women and also some monks who were standing around cheered and cheered, and all the icon lovers claimed a great Christian victory.

We, of course, lament the untimely demise of these soldiers, and wish that the icon could have been defended by less violent strategies. However, any iconoclast—which, of course, means "image breaker"—can expect to have a bad time of it in any age, and rightly so. An iconoclast is a person insufficiently loyal to the popular ideas, idols and mythologies of his particular culture and society. Anyone with even a smattering of sociology knows that you can't have very many people shattering popular images and idols or pretty soon you won't have a stable society. This is why we must not permit a few dissidents to besmirch the image of a J. Edgar Hoover or a Congressman L. Mendel Rivers. This is why we must curb the Ralph Naders before they tarnish the gloss on the idol of big business and our consumer economy.

At any rate, the Christian Corporation became alarmed at the growing iconoclasm which threatened to destroy utterly the whole business of image worship. It called a general council to meet at Nicaea in 787 to consider the problem. Happily, both Roman Christians and Constantinople Christians agreed that icon worship is beneficial to all, and that churches should contain plenty of images. Sad to relate, though, the Council of Nicaea in 787 was the last time the Eastern and Western branches of the Christian Corporation agreed, officially, about anything.

From 787 on, both Roman and Constantinople Christians had

[6] Pope Paul is by all acclaimed an intellectual, and he was much taken aback by the ire of the public when, recently, he said some of the more popular saints may never have existed and abolished their obligatory feast days.

images in their churches. We would assume, then, that the threat of schism had been abated, but it hadn't. A controversy arose between the two branches of the Christian Corporation as to the profound theological significance of flat versus three-dimensional images. The Constantinople Christians claimed that the only truly holy images were flat, or at least no more protuberant than bas-relief. The Roman Christians insisted just as vehemently that fully-rounded, three-dimensional images were every bit as holy as bas-relief or a painting.

We do not wish to take sides in this dispute. Like all large and vital theological issues there is much to be said for both positions, and the arguments are so complex as to require a professional theologian to untangle them. We can see how bas-relief icons could be holier than statuary. On the other hand, three-dimensional images can convey many pious messages. It is a little like the great debate —still raging in some sections of the Christian Corporation—over whether the Almighty prefers clergy and choirs to wear vestments and robes, or if He favors plain business suits and Sunday dresses. Important questions are never easy to decide, and the Eastern and Western branches of the Christian Corporation never did agree on the kind of images acceptable to heaven. It was this disagreement which led to the final break.

CELIBACY OF THE CLERGY DEFENDED

There were some other differences between Roman Christianity and Constantinople Christianity, of course. The Eastern branch believed a clergyman had to wear a beard—an idea we find appalling. Rome, on the other hand, insisted on clean-shaven clergymen with crew cuts, just as we do today. The Eastern Church held it acceptable for any priest but a bishop to be married, whereas the Roman Church stated that the only truly holy man is a celibate man.[6] None of these variations in practice would have

[6] You may think that the concept of a celibate clergy got started because the Roman Church taught that sex is nasty, but you are wrong. It got started because powerful bishops were in the habit of handing down their land and title to their oldest son. This robbed the pope of his prerogative of naming a

been sufficient, though, to split the Corporation. Only the irreconcilable positions on icons could have done that.

The final break came in 1054. That was the year in which the bishop of Constantinople came right out and said that the bishop of Rome wasn't number one, and that dissolved whatever bonds still held the two halves of the Christian Corporation together.[7]

We find little to cheer us in this story of the great picture controversy and the fracturing of the Christian Corporation. We are taught, however, that every dark cloud has a silver lining, so we must look for it here.

While we think that it would have made a better corporation if the East and West had ironed out their differences amicably, it is true that the Eastern branch was increasingly fascinated by mysticism, doctrinal precision, and other such concerns which are peripheral to the real business of the Christian Corporation. The Western branch, on the other hand, spent most of its energies on administration, impressive building projects, raising money, relating itself to the political power structure—doing those things, in fact, which we twentieth-century Christians deem important and desirable. Perhaps the Eastern Church would have been a perpetual burden on the Corporation's back, a continual drag on Christian progress. According to this view, the Eastern Church actually did everyone a favor by removing itself from the mainstream of Christendom, thus permitting the Western Church to go about the business of corporation building unencumbered. We think it is best to look at it this way.

---

new bishop (at the pope's price) whenever an old bishop died. So by saying the clergy couldn't have wives the pope eliminated sons who could inherit. Tying together the concept of holiness and the practice of celibacy was probably some public relations man's idea.

[7] We have made this sound very polite, but it really wasn't. The bishop of Constantinople and the bishop of Rome excommunicated each other, meaning each one said the other one and all his adherents would go to the bad place. Bishops never swear at other bishops, of course, but this is what they do when they want to tell another bishop to go to hell.

XII. *Richard Lionheart, Louis the Pious and the Crusades*

No one can say for certain just when the medieval age commenced. At the time, whenever it was, people did not say, "We are now entering the Middle Ages." A historian, then, can pick his own boundaries for the period. We pick the 1050–1350 segment for our middle ages, and might even chop a few decades off of the latter end because, so far as the Christian Corporation is concerned, this is when its stock hit an all-time high on the big board in the sky.

Let us look briefly at the reasons for claiming that the Christian Corporation shone brighter during the Middle Ages than at any other time.

The Middle Ages, so far as the Church is concerned, started off in dismal fashion. We have just told you about the first great division of the corporation when the Eastern branch split off and went its own way because we are obligated to put in the bad stuff as well as the good stuff.

But from here on the story is just magnificent! It is a story of conquest and consolidation, of construction and cogitation, of energy and piety, of faith and fulfillment. The Middle Ages included the crusades, the building of the Gothic cathedrals, the establishment of the universities, and the *Summa Theologica* of Thomas Aquinas. We can hardly wait to tell you about it.

HOW YOU GOT TO HEAVEN IN THE MIDDLE AGES

People today associate the crusades with Richard Coeur de Lion and Louis the Pious, or St. Louis as he has been called since his canonization, and recall that Peter the Hermit also had a little something to do with them. Hardly anyone remembers that it was Pope Urban II who was the actual kickoff man for the crusades.

As we shall see in a moment, the idea for the crusades came as an inspiration from heaven to Urban II, but there was some background to the project which you need to understand.

Basic to our understanding is the well-known fact that at this period the Holy Land was in the hands of the infidel Turks. It is only natural that Christians resented this with a deep and bitter holy resentment, especially since if you wanted to make a pilgrimage to the Holy Sepulcher the Turks charged you admission.

It may puzzle us as to why Christians a long way from the Holy Land were so hot to go there, but they were. To begin, we must distinguish between our world view and theirs. Put simply, medieval man was much more avid to assure himself a place in paradise than is modern man. While we all want to go to heaven, of course, the weak and sentimental theology to which we have been exposed has taught us to depend on a good-natured, permissive God to let us in. Medieval man was not taken in by such illusions. He knew that Yahweh was full of wrath and fury, and that one lifetime was all too short to fix things with the keeper of the pearly gates. He also knew that the best way to fix things was to make a pilgrimage to a holy place, the holier the place the better, and venerate some sacred relics.

THE CRUSADES AS A MARVELOUS TRAVEL PLAN

To satisfy the demand for a pilgrimage the Church put together a travel package which included (1) a trip to the Holy Land and a visit to the Holy Sepulcher and (2) a chance to venerate Christendom's best-grade relics and maybe get a splinter from the true Cross.[1] Here was a travel package so attractive, as any experienced travel agent will tell you, that it was well-nigh irresistible.[2]

Here also was the ostensible reason for starting the crusades. There were, as there usually are, ancillary motives not of an entirely pious nature. One respected historian sums up the popularity of the crusades, attributing their appeal to (a) love of adventure; (b) hopes for plunder; (c) desire to steal somebody else's land; (d) the pious anxiety about getting to heaven and (e) religious hatred.

We could wish that the crusades had been motivated only by spiritual reasons such as anxiety to get to heaven and religious hatred, but we sadly admit that some worldly aspirations played a part, too, in these great religious campaigns.

One other snippet of history will be helpful to you as you attempt to understand the crusades. One day Pope Urban II was attending to papal business at Piacenza, which is in northern Italy, when some fellows came in to see him and said they were from Constantinople. They said they had been sent by Alexius I, emperor of Constantinople, and that the emperor wanted to start a war against the Turks but as this was impractical without some soldiers to do the fighting, would the pope please send him a regiment or two?

We would have expected Urban to give these clowns the heave-ho, as on the face of it this was an outrageous request, but he didn't. The reason he didn't was that he thought someone should get in a few Christian whacks at the Turks[3] before the Turks decided to sack Rome or do something equally unpleasant. Urban told the fellows they could report to Alexius that he, Urban II,

[1] The true Cross was a very large cross. We know this because splinters from it, duly authenticated and still in existence, would—it is estimated—fill 15½ boxcars, which is a lot of lumber.

[2] It still is. The package has proved so sound that travel agents are still employing it to their enrichment. We don't have to kick the Turks out of the Holy Land any more to make the package practical, but you might get winged by a bomb or shrapnel from the Arab-Israeli war.

[3] Turks are infidels, so God likes it very much when Christians bang them around some.

would recruit some troops for a war on the Turks at the first convenient opportunity.

Now let us journey to the town of Clermont in the province of Auvergne in France. Urban had convened a church council consisting of bishops and abbots, with a few counts and lesser laymen thrown in to beef up the crowd. This was on November 18, 1095. The agenda said the meeting was to settle relations between the Church and Emperor Henry IV of Germany, who was making a nuisance of himself. The meeting droned on for nine days. Everyone was bored silly, so the pope decided to make a speech as he fancied himself to be an exciting speaker. Why not pep things up by launching a campaign to recruit soldiers to fight the Turks, he thought, so he did. We give you here an edited version of what he said.

Soldiers of Christ, he began, things are in a hell of a mess in the Holy Land. The infidel Turks are treating our Christian pilgrims something awful, which is what you might expect because everyone knows that Turks are jerks. Why, for recreation they practice swordsmanship by chopping off Christians' heads, laying wagers as to whether they can do it in one stroke or not, which is shocking because we all know gambling is a sin. So why don't we get organized and go over there and chop us some Turkish necks?

This, of course, stirs our blood, but it didn't do much for the council at Clermont. There was a smattering of applause, but thirteen dukes and four bishops were observed napping, and one archbishop snored out loud. Obviously it was going to take more than a little Turk-baiting to stir this godly council out of its somnolence.

Here is where the inspiration from heaven came in. Urban threw away his manuscript and cut loose with a rabble-rousing appeal to "liberate the precious shrine of the Holy Sepulcher." That did it. The bishop of Le Puy, who was so gouty he could hardly walk from the dinner table to his bedchamber, was the first to volunteer to be a crusader, which earned him a special spot in Christian history and, we hope, also in heaven.[4] Eye-witness ac-

---

[4] Though he was the first to volunteer to go on crusade, there is no record that he ever went.

counts of the event tell us that the crowd came to its feet stomping and shouting, and the meeting broke up in a sort of Christian mob scene.

PLANNING THE HOLY INVASION

The next morning the bishops, who pretty much ran things to suit themselves in those days, got together and drew up rules for the holy invasion against the Turks. It was suggested that all high-class armies wear uniforms and therefore they should hire Pierre Cardin or Bill Blass to design a nifty set of threads for the armies of Christ. Someone pointed out, however, that, as most of the crusaders wouldn't have two dimes to rub together, they would expect the Church to pay for the uniforms. This, the bishops perceived immediately, could run into a lot of bread. The solution, a clever one we think, was to tell the soldiers that they had to have a cross of colored material sewn on their tunics, a plan which reduced the Church's outlay for uniforms to nothing. It is never wise, though, to tell people you are doing something so that they, not you, will have to pay the freight. It is always better to pretend that the increase in price is for the customer's own benefit, as our telephone companies and other giant businesses have learned so well. So what the bishops did was to say that *Crucesignati*, which means "a man with a colored-cloth cross sewn on his tunic," would be the name for anyone going on crusades. The English word for *cruesignati* is "crusader," and that is how the crusades and crusaders got their names.

Another rule the bishops drew up was designed to protect the property of the crusader while he was away. Since the crusaders would be walking to the Holy Land and this would take some little time, it would have been remiss of the council not to have appointed trustees for the care of the farms and money and other worldly goods the crusader left behind, not to mention that he might never get back at all. It was thought best for all concerned to have the bishop of the diocese in which the crusader resided to handle this chore. Apparently not too many bishops planned to go on the crusades themselves, but we must remember that bishops have heavy responsibilities and it is difficult for them to get away.

A crusader's vow was adopted which read that a crusader promised on his sacred honor to kick the stuffing out of the infidels. If a crusader chickened out after he had started he would be excommunicated, which is a pretty awful thing to have happen to you. On the other hand, if you got skewered by a Turk or caught a fatal case of the measles while on crusade your sins were automatically forgiven. These provisions were an added inducement to sign up, something like a stock option or a Christmas bonus.

The date of the crusade (no one then dreamed that it would take more than one) was set for the Feast of the Assumption, which was August 15, 1096, and a good eight months hence. However, when a movement of such magnitude is on the drawing board, some idiot is bound to become overenthusiastic and jump the gun. In this case the idiot was Peter the Hermit. Peter the Hermit's name may not have been Peter. A hermit he wasn't, at least not very much of the time, because he nearly always had hundreds of people trailing around after him. Probably he was called the Hermit because he was such a shabby dresser and had a scraggly beard and didn't bathe very often if ever, all characteristics associated in the popular mind with hermits and men of extraordinary holiness. What he did was to start preaching the crusades, which was O.K., but he was so enraptured by his own oratory that he decided to start his own crusade long before the agreed-upon date.

Our scholarly research has laid bare Peter the Hermit's motives in this precipitous action. He had tried, some years earlier, to visit Jerusalem, but had been roughed up by the Turks. We do not doubt that he was itching to have a go at the Turks for the good Christian reason that they were infidels. But he was also egged on by a desire for personal revenge, which we all know is not a good Christian reason, but a motive not always easy to suppress, even for good Christians.

Peter's success at rounding up volunteers would make a modern

U. S. Army recruiter blush with shame. He assembled, by the power of his preaching and buttonholing everyone he saw, an army of maybe thirty thousand. It wasn't the most efficient fighting force the world has ever seen. Most of Peter's crusaders were gullible peasants, with a few raggedy knights under the leadership of Sir Walter the Penniless to lend the expedition what little class it had.

PETER THE HERMIT'S SHABBY CRUSADE

Peter's crusaders slouched across Europe, stealing their food and swiping things for souvenirs to take home to the wife and kids. They also massacred a few hundred Jews here and there, and in other ways made a damn nuisance of themselves.

When they got to the territory of the Emperor Alexius, he saw that these crusaders, brave Christian soldiers that they may have been, were not exactly what he had in mind when he asked the pope to send some regiments. However, he helped the crusaders establish themselves in an old fort on the shores of the Gulf of Nicomedia not far from the Turks. It was, in fact, much too close to the Turks, who galloped in one night and butchered all but about three thousand of the crusaders, and that was the end of the first attempt to liberate the Holy Sepulcher.[5]

When the genuine first crusade got going, it turned into a spectacular success! It took a couple of years or so, but on July 15, 1099, the crusaders took Jerusalem and rescued the Holy Sepulcher. This was one occasion on which the Christians really skunked the Turks. We are borrowing the following glorious account from H. Daniel-Rops as contained in his monumental work *Cathedral and Crusade:*

"Thousands [of Christians] . . . behaved themselves like butchers. At the Mosque of Omar, which stands on the sight of the temple, there was such slaughter that the blood ran ankle-deep. Hours passed before the intoxication of unbridled rage gave place once

[5] It was not, however, the end of Peter the Hermit as he had thoughtfully remained in Constantinople, quite a way from any actual combat.

more to Christian faith. Towards dusk the conquerors, now washed and recovered from their insane fury, climbed the Via Dolorosa barefooted, devoutly kissing each place where Christ had fallen. Then they flung themselves upon the ground before the Holy Sepulchre, their arms stretched out cross-wise, and lay there a long while, happy if exhausted."[6]

We assure you that dozens of equally inspiring stories of the battle of Jerusalem exist, all illustrating the holy fervor and Christian zeal of the crusaders. We would quote some more of them, but it might make you too nostalgic for the good old days.

We can't go into detail about the whole crusade movement because it lasted nearly two hundred years. The history of crusades gets to be rather repetitive anyway. After the success of the first crusade, the Christians set up the Kingdom of Jerusalem and took the attitude that they were there permanently. But they weren't. As soon as the crusaders would go home, leaving only a small garrison to defend the city, the Turks—a treacherous lot—would come back and clobber the Christians. This would necessitate another crusade to rescue the Holy Sepulcher. It is no mean feat to calculate the actual number of crusades because some of them didn't amount to much while others did. There were six to eight main ones, if you don't count Frederick II and his sixth crusade as a main one, which some historians do and some don't.

Frederick, at the time he went on crusade, wasn't really a Christian because he had been excommunicated. When the pope heard about Frederick's crusade he is reported to have shouted, "He's no crusader, he's a pirate!" Much to the embarrassment of Christendom, though, Frederick had things settled in no time. Not being a passionate Christian he wasn't as interested in exterminating the infidel as he should have been, so he slipped a little cash to the right people and worked out a diplomatic settlement which returned Jerusalem to the Christians, freed the Christian prisoners, and said people of any faith were free to pray wherever they pleased whenever they pleased. Frederick considered diplomatic negotiation at

---

[6] We are told that the next day the Christians were ashamed that they had been quite so rough with the infidels.

least as Christian as fighting, and it did save wear and tear on the troops.

Christendom, naturally, screamed that Frederick was guilty of treason, sacrilege and impiety, and started another crusade even though there was nothing to prevent Christians from praying at the Holy Sepulcher.

THE CHILDREN'S CRUSADE COMES TO NAUGHT

We suppose it is necessary, too, to tell you about the children's crusades, although we'd rather not. A French kid named Stephen, who obviously needed professional help, had a vision which he interpreted as God's command to drum up an army of youngsters and God would see to it that the juvenile task force captured the Holy Sepulcher.

A German kid named Nicholas heard about what the French kid was doing and decided to get in on the act. Each of these young Christian generals collected several thousand adolescents and set out, by separate paths, to the Holy Land.

Nicholas' army made it through Switzerland and over the Alps, although a good many of them froze to death on the way, and into Italy. From Italy they expected to walk to Asia Minor because Nicholas said the sea would part for them, but it didn't, and what was left of the crusade settled down and became Italians.

Stephen led his section of the children's crusade to the port of Marseilles where he, too, counted on the sea to roll back and let his kids walk to the Holy Land without getting their feet wet. The sea, however, seemed to be in no hurry to part and Stephen was in a hurry, so he arranged to go by boat. Some of the boats were wrecked, and others had unscrupulous captains who sold the kids into slavery to Mohammedans and worse, and that was the end of that. The children's crusade is not pointed out as one of the more edifying and productive movements in Christian history.

The story of the crusades is sprinkled with names synonymous with faith and valor. Godfrey de Bouillon, Baldwin I, king of Jerusalem, Frederick Barbarossa, Hugh de Payens, who founded

the Templars, and a host of others. Two names, both riveted to
the crusades in the public mind, outsparkle all others. They are
Richard the Lionhearted and Louis the Pious.

COEUR DE LION

Before the onset of effete times such as ours, with their cynicism
about deeds of derring-do and lack of respect for the truly heroic,
Richard Coeur de Lion was the very model of the warrior king,
one of the few figures capable of eliciting interest and admiration
from bored schoolboys listlessly picking over the pages of history.

The author of *Itinerarium Regis Ricardi,* thought to have been
Coeur de Lion's chaplain, tells us that "He was lofty of stature, of
a shapely build, with hair halfway between red and yellow.[7] His
limbs were straight and flexible . . . Not only could he claim the
loftiest position and praise in virtue of his noble birth, but also by
reason of his virtues . . . his splendid achievements would throw
a shade over the greatest praise we could give them . . . the lord
of the ages had given him such generosity of soul and endued him
with such virtues that he seemed rather to belong to earlier times
than these . . . His was the valor of Hector, the magnanimity of
Achilles; he was no whit . . . inferior to Alexander, or less than
Roland in manhood."

Richard sewed the cross cloth of the crusader on his tunic early
in life. He was only thirty-two when he became king, and he wore
the crucesignati at the coronation. We are a little dismayed to
learn that, though Richard talked a great deal about going on
crusade, he appeared to be in no hurry to go. Some people at the
time actually joked about his seeming reluctance to get cracking
and rescue the Holy Sepulcher. But he finally did go. This was the
third crusade, the one historians regard as by all means the best-
organized, the best-fought, the most glorious crusade of all.[8] The only
real flaw in the enterprise was that it failed of its objective because

---

[7] Which would have made his hair a flaming orange, but we suspect that it
was some other shade the chaplain had in mind.

[8] What historians mean by such encomiums is that the third crusade was
somewhat less of a disaster than the others.

the Moslems just sat in Jerusalem and beat off every invasion launched by the Christians.

In other ways, though, it was an unarguable success. A part of the enterprise was the siege of the city of Acre. A siege is where you and your army sit down outside a walled city and try to reduce the army inside to abject surrender by starving them out. Every so often you attack the city and fight some battles, then, when everybody gets tired you go back to sitting around some more. It is obvious that a siege can be pretty dull, a fact not lost on the British merchant class. During the siege of Acre, merchants and bankers set up business in Richard's camp and imported entertainers to lure customers. It was something like a permanent county fair. Between battles the Moslem soldiers would come out to Richard's camp and buy things and watch the jugglers and puppet shows and get drunk with Richard's brave crusaders. Then, when it was time to fight another battle, the Moslems would go back to their besieged city, and Moslems and Christians would fall to slaughtering each other again.

Since warfare today is carried on so clearly and efficiently with bombs and machine guns and automatic rifles and napalm, it is not easy for us to imagine how messy it was at the time of the crusades. Stories of the third crusade, for example, abound in accounts of battles where the field was strewn with severed heads and limbs. It was in such glorious combat as this that Richard distinguished himself. He had exceedingly long arms, and with his longsword was able to whack an enemy before the enemy could get close enough to whack him. "Cutting a swath with his sword," and "leaving a path behind him paved with those slain by his good right arm" are phrases characteristic of the historians of the time when describing the king's exploits on the field of battle. Because of his bravery and prowess in the battles of the third crusade, he was nicknamed "Richard with the heart of a lion," and the name has stuck to him down through history.[9]

We would have to say that the crusades were worth it if they

---

[9] Some people say that he wasn't called lionheart until a ballad of the fourteenth century depicts him killing a lion by tearing out its heart. But since this same ballad also says he once ate a young and tender Turk for supper, we are inclined to look on the whole tale as apocryphal.

had done no more than produce the romantic hero figure of Richard Coeur de Lion to serve as a model and guide and inspiration to succeeding generations. No one else conjures up in our imaginations the ideal wise British Christian virtuous brave devout hero king as does Richard.

It is true, we admit, that he wasn't British but French. He spent no more than six months in Britain in his whole life, and that was only to raise money. He never did learn to speak English. He wasn't always as wise as he might have been as a king either. Historian Sir James Ramsay says he was a crook in the means to which he resorted to raise money and a fool in the spending of it.

No one, we are happy to say, denies that Richard was a Christian, but not a few deny that he was devout. Some say he was famed for his picturesque swearing. Others tell us he was chaste so far as girls were concerned, not bothering them at all, but that he was an avowed, confessed and practicing homosexual. Also they say he drank like a fish and was a rotten administrator.

When he died, his career as king, we are sorry to report, got mixed reviews by the critics. One of them, Gaucelin Faidit by name, evaluated Coeur de Lion this way: "A thousand years shall never see his peer, so openhanded, noble, brave and generous."[10] Berthan de Born, on the other hand, wrote of Richard's reign that "Venom, avarice, crime, unbounded lust, foul famine, atrocious pride, blind desire, have reigned for twice five years." We have here, obviously, some discrepancy of judgment. But then we should not be too surprised. Senator Goldwater and the president of NBC don't agree entirely on Spiro T. Agnew either.

anything but the best about Louis. He was a model Christian, a

LOUIS THE PIOUS

Coeur de Lion passed on in April of the year 1199. Fortunately there was another Christian warrior-hero waiting in the wings to take up the mantle. This was Louis IX of France, or Louis the Pious, or St. Louis. You are hard put to find a historian who says

[10] Richard had bailed Gaucelin out when his creditors were breathing down his neck, so it is possible this appraisal of the king is not entirely objective.

model king, a model husband, a model father, and a model crusader.

As a Christian, he had what seemed to many—then or now—the odd idea that your faith should govern every aspect of your life. Only a handful of people in any age care to go to such extremes with their Christianity, and hardly any kings do it. That is why Louis is such a towering historical figure, like Wilt Chamberlain.

As a husband, he is a standout. He was married to Margaret of Provence, a flaky dame who thought Louis was much too religious for his own good. Their union, one historian says "was little more than a prolonged and often painful misunderstanding." Most guys living under such conditions take to drink, or console themselves with mistresses, or maybe both. But not Louis. He stuck with Margaret and had eleven children. He tried hard to bring his children up as good Christians.[11]

If Louis was less than perfect, it was as a King. Not that he didn't try hard to be a good Christian king. He did. But he was too far to the left for our tastes, believing that serfs should be freed, that minorities should be treated with scrupulous fairness, and that a poor man was just as good as a rich man. It is fortunate for him that there was no John Birch Society back then or it would have nailed his hide to the wall, along with President Eisenhower's, as a comsymp. He was overly demanding about honesty in his judges, too. He absolutely forbade conflict of interest in his judges, an attitude which would dismay President Nixon,[12] and he wouldn't even let them frequent taverns or shoot crap.

Louis did not get in on the attempt to rescue the Holy Sepulcher until about 1248, which was fairly late in the day for crusading. In 1244 he fell desperately ill, and took an oath to go on crusade if he recovered. He recovered, but there wasn't any crusade going on at the moment, so he had to wait around until the pope could get another one started. Louis fought his first crusade battle at

[11] For a Christian present one year he sent his favorite daughter a book of Christian discipline and a hair shirt. It is unlikely that the gift of a hair shirt would thrill a modern teen-age girl, but we must remember that styles were different back then.

[12] Like President Nixon he wanted to reduce taxes, but—again like President Nixon—he couldn't because of a costly war. France had to finance most of the crusades, and the crusades sopped up money almost as fast as Vietnam.

Damietta in Egypt on June 4, 1249. His army had some initial success but it didn't last, and Louis was taken prisoner. As a prisoner he was a big hit with the Egyptians, converting many of them to Christianity. The Sultan finally let him go home. This was in 1254.

Louis never forgave himself for failing to liberate Jerusalem, and vowed to try again, which he did with the eighth crusade as it is sometimes counted, in 1270. To spare you the painful details, let us just say that the eighth crusade was a fiasco, and Louis caught cholera in Tunis and died August 25, 1270.

IN DEFENSE OF CHRISTIAN WARS

Before we evaluate the crusades we feel it necessary to explain the Christian Corporation's attitude toward war. Thoughtless and ill-intentioned folk occasionally infer from the length and ferocity of the crusades that the Church in those days heartily approved of military endeavors and bloodshed. Nothing could be further from the truth.

As a matter of fact, the Church had been trying, for many years prior to the crusades, to put a damper on the incessant wars that plagued society. In those days, counts and dukes and the like were forever fighting each other and knocking down each other's castles and swiping each other's cattle and women. Their troops kept tromping up the land, making it hard to grow anything, not to mention the time and effort and money diverted into these ubiquitous battles. The Church kept saying they should cut out such foolishness, but the nobles went right on fighting anyway.

What the Christian Corporation did then was to decide that it was unreasonable, in the light of original sin, to expect no wars at all. So it took steps to turn these big, expensive wars into small, cheap wars. It instituted what it called the "Peace of God," which didn't require renouncing war and fighting and plunder, but it did try to limit them to reasonable amounts.

The first rule for fighting as laid down by the Peace of God was, quite naturally, that there would be no attacks on church property.

The second rule was that there would be no attacks on the clergy. Also, the rules said, it would be better if you didn't mess with cattle, farming equipment, or pilgrims.[13] Another rule said you really shouldn't despoil merchants or horse around with the women of any duke or earl you conquered.

The Peace of God didn't work very well as it exempted too many targets. The Christian Corporation then tried another tack, which it called the "Truce of God." This program relaxed somewhat the stringent rules of the Peace of God. It said it was O.K. to fight and pillage except no battles were to be fought from Wednesday evening until Monday morning, and no wars at all during Advent and Lent. The Truce of God was, we can see, a much sounder plan, but it didn't work very well either.

Finally the Church wised up to the fact that men really enjoy putting on a uniform and whooping off to battle and despoiling women and swiping someone else's property and sitting around campfires telling dirty stories. They like this much better than being accountants or carpenters or insurance agents and going to mass every Sunday and being dominated by their wives. So the Church said if Christians just had to fight it would be better for everybody in general and the Church in particular if they quit fighting other Christians and fought infidels such as the Turks. Now that you understand the background you can reconcile in your mind the disparate facts that the Christian Corporation was foursquare for peace and amity, but that it also beat the drums for the wars of the crusades. It makes us feel much better about the whole business of the crusades.

WERE THE CRUSADES WORTH THE TROUBLE?

When we attempt to assess the crusades we are in a quandary, and with little help from the historians. Even among Christian historians estimates of the value of the crusades vary widely. M. Olichas, in his work *Missions* is indecisive. *The History of*

---

[13] Pilgrims, as we know, are usually welcome because they bring money into the economy.

Catholic Missions by B. de Vaulx lacks enthusiasm. Funk-Brentano's book *The Crusades* is downright gloomy. Another, whom we prefer not to name, says the crusades were "a lunatic business."

H. Daniel-Rops, on the other hand, espouses the positive view. He fairly gurgles with rapture as he contemplates them. In *Cathedral and Crusade* he writes: "In the heart of every man born of Christ the crusades remain a glorious memory; and it is significant that the very word 'crusade' still suggests a heroic enterprise undertaken for some pure and lofty purpose. As long as Christianity endures on earth, as long as there exists a civilization from which Christian principles have not been wholly banished, there will be men to treasure these pages of sanctity and heroism inscribed by the crusaders with their blood."

How, then, shall we render a verdict? Perhaps logic, fairness, and objectivity require us to total up the gains and losses and strike a balance.

Let us look at the good part first.

All competent historians are agreed that the crusades were ideally suited for expanding the import-export business. They enriched countless stalwart Christians. They introduced shallots, which are really Ascalon onions, to the West, and no true gourmet in Christendom would think the crusades too high a price to pay for what otherwise would be a shallotless cuisine.

The crusades were great for people who had never been anywhere or seen anything. It can be said with little fear of contradiction that the crusades were the largest stimulus to the travel business prior to the invention of the jet plane and the fifteen-countries-in-twenty-one-days touring package.

There were, too, some spectacular spin-offs from the crusades. The Knights Templars and the Hospitalers were products of these Christian wars.[14] So was the Order of St. Dominic.

---

[14] The Hospitalers actually got started earlier, but they never amounted to much until the crusades.

THE BAD STUFF LISTED

Before we are overcome with elation in contemplation of the blessings brought by the crusades we must look at the debit side of the ledger.

No reliable figures are available as to the number of people killed as a result of the crusades, but it had to be a staggering total. It was in the hundreds of thousands, and compares quite favorably to the numbers we are able to slaughter in our modern, efficient, non-theological wars. This, perhaps, is not to be viewed entirely as a liability, because overpopulation was getting to be a problem even then, and the crusades did help to reduce the surplus.

There were also thousands of people who came home minus legs, arms, eyes and what not, just as from modern battles, and we can't find any advantage in this at all.

We have to think of what the crusades cost in money, too. While it wouldn't keep a modern crusade, such as our current effort in Vietnam, going but for a few days, the amount was still awesome. It well-nigh bankrupt the Christian Corporation as well as France.

Worst of all, of course, was that the crusades failed of their objective, which was to capture the Holy Land, especially the Holy Sepulcher, so that Christians could go there freely and pray whenever they wanted to.[15]

MAKING OUR EVALUATION

How are we to decide, then, if the crusades were a success or a failure? Did they write a glorious page in the history of the Christian Corporation, or were they a lunatic enterprise from start to finish?

Judged by the thesis of this book, which is that anything which ultimately helped the Christian Corporation is good, and anything

[15] After the crusades petered out, Christians had no difficulty whatever in negotiating an agreement with the infidels that Christians could visit the Holy Land and pray at the sacred shrines whenever they pleased.

which hurt it is bad—and we think this is the only valid and applicable standard—the crusades constitute one of the great success stories of all times.

Look, for example, at the public relations value of the crusades. Never before, or since, has one simple idea been able to whip the faithful into a frenzy for God and country and keep them steamed up for two hundred years.

The crusades taught the Corporation much. A signal lesson from them is that, although the stated purpose of any popular religious movement is seldom, if ever, realized, this is really irrelevant. The actual value of any Christian crusade, ancient or modern, is not that it achieves anything tangible in the way of results, but that it generates enthusiasm for the Christian Corporation. The Holy Land may have remained unclaimed, and the crusaders may have failed to kill enough Mohammedans to make a dent in them, and the whole works may have cost a wad of dough. Trifles, really. What did matter was that out of them—so historians say—came a sense of unity in the Christian Corporation and a vision of all Christendom united under the leadership of the chairman of the Corporation.

In short, the Church went into the crusades a large and prosperous, but disorganized and inefficient business. It came out of them a giant, united corporation. By anyone's standards, results like this spell a smashing success!

XIII. *The Gothic cathedral—or the Christian Corporation builds a home office at last*

Professor C. Northcote Parkinson, that eminent chronicler of mankind's triumphs and follies, tells us in his work *In-Laws and Outlaws* that, sooner or later, every corporation wants to build a spectacular home office. During the years of expansion a corporation doesn't worry much about what its plant looks like, Professor Parkinson relates. However, with maturity and success come a sense of corporate pride. There is a concern to express the corporate image in stone and marble and glass.

We look on this edifice urge as laudable, and are glad to be able to tell you that it came over the Christian Corporation just as it afflicted Seagram, Pan-Am, and John Hancock, except earlier, of course.

Recall that we told you in an earlier chapter that in its pre-corporation days the Church had no buildings at all. It carried on its activities in someone's house, or a cave, or outdoors in a field or on a hillside. We are alarmed by a movement among what we refer to as "renewalites" and other avant-garde Christian groups today to regress to this primitive practice of carrying on the Christian community without any special Christian buildings. History shows us, after all, that the early Christians built their own buildings just as soon as they could get around to it.[1]

[1] The oldest Christian church we know about was unearthed in the ruins of the city of Dura on the Euphrates River and was built, we think, about A.D. 232. However, don't rush off to Dura to see it, because it now reposes in the Art Museum of Yale University.

To condense a lot of Christian architectural history, churches were small at first, but as the Corporation prospered they got bigger and fancier. By the year A.D. 1000 what we now call Romanesque architecture was the most popular and prevalent style for churches.[2]

THE DEFICIENCIES OF ROMANESQUE CHURCHES

The first Romanesque churches were rather solid and squat in appearance. Some of them were even round. In Romanesque architecture the walls support the weight of the roof, and since the roof is a stone vault, you have to have pretty thick walls with hardly any windows in them, just a few fenestrations. This is why Romanesque buildings tend to resemble elegant prisons. Also, Romanesque churches were awfully dark inside with just flickering candles for illumination, so the atmosphere was rather spooky. The Christian theology of the time was rather spooky too, so the church buildings accurately reflected the prevailing point of view, but Romanesque churches are not places you want to hang around for hours on end.

We know that it is in the nature of corporations to put up bigger and bigger buildings as business grows. The Christian Corporation kept putting up bigger and bigger Romanesque churches, but the stone-vaulted roofs got so heavy that they forced the supporting walls outward and the churches collapsed, which gets to be discouraging after a while.[3] Sometimes they would put wooden roofs on the churches, but they were forever catching fire from some stray spark or bolt of lightning, so this wasn't much of an improvement.

Fortunately for the Christian Corporation, the invention of Gothic architecture coincided with its urge to build vast, soaring, overwhelming home-office buildings. We can't pinpoint the date, but it was sometime early in the Middle Ages.

[2] Architectural scholars say the Romanesque style combines influences from Byzantium, Eastern Asia, and Islam, not to mention touches traceable to the Scythian and Sarmatian steppes. It was only natural, then, to call it Romanesque.

[3] The large Romanesque abbey church at Bec collapsed three times in a hundred years.

UNDERSTANDING GOTHIC ARCHITECTURE

There are several ways to visualize a Gothic church. One way is to think of it as a huge prehistoric animal with its skeleton on the outside where its skin would normally be, and its skin on the inside where its skeleton would normally be. This plan probably wouldn't be ideal for an animal, but it works awfully well for a church.

Another way to envision a Gothic church is to imagine that it is a shaky old shed with its walls propped up by poles. If you have enough poles and they are stuck firmly enough in the ground you can make the walls of the shed ever so high and the walls won't fall down, even if the roof is awfully heavy. This is because the roof of the shed presses on the walls, and the walls—instead of collapsing—press on the poles. The poles then press on the ground, which is solid enough to bear all the weight you are likely to need. We have now told you all you need to know about the engineering principles of Gothic architecture.

Now that you have a mastery of the technical aspects of Gothic architecture you will have no trouble imagining the mind-blowing innovations possible to it.

There is, for example, the expansion of the windows. Since the walls of a Gothic church serve little purpose except to keep the rain out you can make them mostly of glass if you want to. Then, if you make your windows out of little bits of colored glass leaded together, you not only get a very pretty color effect, but it is also possible to arrange the bits of glass into pictures of saints and animals and religious symbols, getting also a very nice pious effect.

Gothic churches can be very small or very large, of course, but the tendency of the Christian Corporation has always been to make them as large as possible. The Cathedral of St. John the Divine in Manhattan, the world's largest Gothic church, encloses space ample for the New York Jets and the Oakland Raiders to play in if the weather ever gets too bad at Shea Stadium, although a running back might have to dodge around a pillar now and then on an end sweep.

Inventing Gothic architecture, difficult as that was, was by no means the most formidable task confronting the Christian Corporation in its endeavor to erect a suitable home office. Any experienced pastor will tell you that designing a new church is the easier part of the task. The tough part of any church building program is raising the money. Fortunately, accounts of how the Gothic builders promoted their projects have come down to us. Their methods, it turns out, were startlingly similar to the methods a congregation would employ in carrying out such a scheme today.

HOW THE MONEY WAS RAISED

Back then, as now, someone has to get the idea that a new church building is required. Back then, as now, it was nearly always the clergy which first became aware of the need for a new church. The clergy, being by nature and calling more spiritual than the laity, perceives the need for larger and more magnificent edifices for the glory of God when the laity is still content with the sturdy, serviceable buildings they already have.[4]

Imagine that you were living in a cathedral town in the twelfth or thirteenth century. You, as a layman, had never given a thought to the building of a new cathedral because there is nothing wrong, structurally, with the old one. Pretty soon, though, you notice references in sermons to the need for a new cathedral, little hints that maybe God is mortified with the plain, shabby, out-of-date building in which you are now worshiping. The primary reason given for building a new church, then or now, is always the greater glory of God, as of course it should be.

Before long, the sermons at the cathedral would give other than pious reasons why a new building was needed. Local pride was one

---

[4] Notre Dame's builders had to wreck a church on the site which was good for another 500 years. Bishop Walter de Mortagne tore down his almost new Romanesque cathedral because everyone was going Gothic and he wanted to go along with the trend. William de Seignelay, bishop of Auxerre, explained that he leveled his perfectly good non-Gothic cathedral to put up a Gothic one because he had seen a dandy Gothic cathedral in Paris and wanted one like it.

reason always given. The clergy usually thought it prudent, also, to mention the economic advantages which would accrue to a community with the foresight to finance a large new Gothic cathedral. Not only would it provide work for local artisans, but people from all over would come to see the new cathedral, especially if it contained a representative collection of the efficacious relics of saints, which it nearly always did because saints' relics were in rather generous supply back then. This economic appeal was what we would call hustling for the tourist trade, but in those days the customers were called pilgrims.

Anyway, after a certain amount of such preaching, everyone would be saying, "Yes, of course we need a new cathedral. Anybody can see that."

Today, when the decision to build a new church is made, the congregation usually hires a professional money-raiser to come in and carry on a financial campaign. They may or may not have had professional money-raisers in the Middle Ages, but the way they went about it then is very similar to the way the pros do it now.

The first step in such a venture is to draw up what we call "the advance gift list." All prospects on the advance gift list are known to be loaded, and quite capable of making an enormous contribution to the building project, although not all of them do so. In the Middle Ages the advance gift list for the building of a new cathedral was always headed by the king. The king could usually be counted on for a generous amount because, for political reasons, he couldn't very well get out of it.

After the king came the rich townfolk, local nobility, the bishop of the diocese, and the like. Then, when the big dough was safely in the bag the ordinary folk were invited to participate.

Another favorite way of financing a new church building, then as now, was to designate such items as windows and altarware as "memorial gifts." This means that whoever pays for them can have his name on them. Donors look on memorial gifts as a double bargain—they receive all the spiritual benefits attendant upon giving to the Church and at the same time memorialize themselves.

THE PROSTITUTES' GUILD CONTRIBUTES

The only people not permitted to contribute to a Gothic cathedral were "public sinners."[5] However, there was often a way around this dilemma if the contribution was too large to pass up. When the prostitutes' guild of Paris offered to give Notre Dame a stained glass window, a theologian was appointed to study the matter and see if the gift could be accepted. His recommendation was that the gift should be accepted, but that for public relations reasons the transaction should be handled "unobtrusively."

The Christian Corporation is much more sensitive about this sort of thing today, and of course would be shocked at the very idea of permitting a prostitutes' guild to contribute to the building of a church. Members of the Mafia are noted for their generosity to the Church, we admit, but they give not as a gangsters' guild but as private businessmen. Any fair-minded person can readily see that there is no comparison between accepting a gift to the Church made by a gangster-businessman personally, and accepting a gift from a guild of prostitutes.[6]

Anyway, the Gothic churches got built in great numbers during the Middle Ages. Today, the Gothic church is widely recognized as one of mankind's supreme achievements, but it was not always so. We haven't told you who invented Gothic because no one knows for sure. We do know it got started in France, but it wasn't called French because many effete admirers of fussy Renaissance architecture thought it was crude and vulgar, a "confused heap of eccentricities" as one critic of the style put it. So these critics looked around for a word which meant crude and vulgar to apply to the new architecture. In those days the word "Goth" referred to a barbarous person, so they nicknamed the new architecture "Gothic,"

[5] There was no prohibition against contributions by private sinners.
[6] The author once heard the president of a Christian college defend a gift from a dubious source by saying that the only thing wrong with tainted money is that "it 'taint enough." We may be sure, however, that he is the exception and not the rule among administrators of the modern Christian Corporation.

thinking that everyone would laugh uproariously at their clever joke. But the joke was on the critics, as it often is, because Gothic architecture turned out to be one of those things mankind produces about every thousand years—something that nearly everyone likes.

People who know about such matters tell us that Gothic architecture is at the same time both material and spiritual, bound to the earth but appearing to soar heavenward, a perfect marriage of technology and art, a never-surpassed expression of man, imprisoned by his roots in this world, striving for life in the next world—and many other fine compliments too numerous to mention.

The Christian Corporation set out to build an appropriate home office, and achieved one of the four or five most glorious monuments to the spirit of mankind in all of human history. We can't think of any other corporation that can come even close to matching this record.

XIV. *The Church learns how to handle heretics —Innocent III institutes the Inquisition*

The Holy Office, or the Inquisition as it is popularly known, has had a bad press for several centuries now. People who know little about it associate the Inquisition with torture, and burnings at the stake, and heretics being drawn and quartered, and a number of other distasteful practices. While it is true that, on occasion, the Inquisition resorted to rather vigorous measures to protect the purity of the faith, these are not things we ought to remember about it. To see it as a cruel and inhuman instrument seldom surpassed for man's savage treatment of his fellow man is to see it in distorted perspective. We are certain that, after we have explained it to you, you will look on the Holy Office as not only a necessary and beneficent undertaking, but as one of the inspired strategies of the Christian Corporation. It was the most effective method for handling heretics ever devised by the mind of man.

We have delineated for you the magnificence of the medieval Christian Corporation as an institution and an organization, but we have not mentioned much about the glories of its intellectual achievements. We can no longer postpone mentioning them, though, because you have to understand the Church's concept of truth in order to understand the necessity for the Inquisition.

THE SUPERIORITY OF REVEALED TRUTH

Briefly, the Church—through study and reflection over the centuries—had learned that truth is very similar to two streams. One stream is the truth that men discover by observation, experimentation and the like. The other stream is the truth of divine revelation. But these are not streams of the same size and importance. The stream of humanly discovered truth is only a trickle compared to the broad and placid expanse of the stream of revealed truth.

Now it sometimes happens that the stream of human discovery runs counter to the stream of revelation. Men will think they discover something which contravenes revealed truth. The Church, of course, knows better. It only stands to reason that revealed truth is always true, the Church patiently explains, because truth of divine origin has to be accurate or it wouldn't be divine, so let us have no nonsense about human truth refuting divine revelation. Since truth of divine origin is always revealed through channels in the Christian Corporation, the Corporation is charged with the solemn task of preserving its purity, which is only right.

But some people persist in capriciously insisting on the superiority of the truth they think they have discovered over the revealed truth the Church knows to be true. To permit this, the Church is aware, is to permit the lovely, fragrant waters of divine truth to be polluted. And, as we of the twentieth century should know, pollution should never be permitted or the cleanup job will be long and expensive.

So let us think of the Holy Office, or the Inquisition, as a battle against spiritual and intellectual pollution. Since pollution is such a horrible thing, then we should not be upset that drastic measures often are required to prevent it, or to tidy up the mess it has made. If you have grasped our argument, then you now have the correct perspective on the Inquisition.

The name of Tomás de Torquemada comes to mind most readily when we think of the Inquisition, but historically he came along rather late in the day. It was Pope Innocent III who, around A.D. 1200, conceived of a special department of the Corporation with

no task other than to hunt out and deal with heresy. It was called
the Holy Office, and its employees carried the title "Inquisitors of
the Faith."[1]

THE MILD METHODS OF THE INQUISITION

In the beginning, the methods employed and penalties imposed by
the Inquisition were quite mild and reasonable, considering the
heinous nature of the offense. The heretic's property was confiscated,
of course.[2] The accused heretic could hold no office, nor claim any
of the rights of citizenship. If he was sick or starving no one could
extend to him normal Christian charity under pain of excommunication themselves. Everyone was supposed to shun an exposed heretic.
When he died, the heretic was denied Christian burial.

GNOSTICS AND OTHER PESTS

Early in the thirteenth century southern France was a serpent's
nest of heretics. There was a goodly number of Gnostics living
there, and since you have met the Gnostics in a previous chapter
we don't need to point out again how offensive they were. Then
there were communities of Cathars, and Cathars are really only
Gnostics by another name. Add to these numerous Manichaens and
Arians, both of which are already known to you, plus Waldenses
and *Boni Homines,* who were sort of pre-Lutheran Protestants, and
you can envision the magnitude of the problem facing the Christian

[1] The ability to select names for departments and titles for job categories,
is one sure mark of the able executive. A lesser man than Innocent probably would have set up a "Department for the Suppression of Heresy" and
called its employees "Inspectors of Christian Conformity." While sacrificing
a little something in accuracy, "the Holy Office" and "Inquisitors of the
Faith" sound so much better than these other titles, or any alternatives we
can think of for that matter.

[2] No one can think it unjust that the heretic should bear the expense involved in ferreting him out because—once apprehended—heretics would often
recant, thus restoring them to the blessings of an orthodox relationship to
the Christian Corporation, a gift which, of course, is beyond price.

Corporation. No halfway measures softened by mercy were capable of solving it.

It was not until the Inquisition was put in the hands of the Dominican friars that any real progress was made. The Dominicans, who knew that heresy is the sin of sins, the most odious of all transgressions, saw more clearly than even Innocent III that one mustn't be queasy about methods of extirpating it. They drew up a constitution which stated that once a heretic had been officially excommunicated he was to be turned over to the State, which would then proceed to burn him. The same thing would happen to non-heretics who sheltered or defended a heretic. Children of heretics were to be denied the right to hold public office through the second generation.[3] There were other provisions to cover other contingencies, but the above penalties proved marvelously effective for curbing theological deviation, discouraging non-conformity, and keeping everyone loyal to the Christian Corporation.

TOMÁS DE TORQUEMADA PERFECTS THE HOLY OFFICE

It remained for Tomás de Torquemada, though, to bring the Holy Office to its highest perfection of efficiency. We must tell you a little about this remarkable man.

He was born in the kingdom of Castile, the most important of those kingdoms which made up what we now know as Spain, in 1420. His early life was very dull, so we can skip over most of it. To sum it up concisely, even as a young lad he exhibited an unusual talent for piety and the study of common law. He became a Dominican friar and rose to modest eminence, becoming headman at a monastery in Segovia, where he distinguished himself at administration and self-abnegation.[4]

---

[3] An exception was made for children who were themselves not guilty of heresy and who publicly condemned the iniquity of their fathers. This rule tended to inhibit free and easy family conversation.

[4] He wore a hair shirt, used rough woolen blankets in place of sheets, and never ate meat. The other monks at Segovia thought his piety excessive, as not all Christians, even monks, wish to carry self-denial this far. But we say if you have a gift for suffering, why not use it?

During these quiet years of meditation and prayer and constant asceticism, Torquemada developed the marvelous, monstrous passions which were to make him one of history's best-remembered figures. Being a Dominican, he longed for the Holy Office to be established and flourishing in his native land where, through lack of sufficient piety on the part of the various kings, it hadn't even been instituted. He also longed for a united Spain. The best way to unite Spain, he perceived, was through the Inquisition.

It was not until he was fifty-eight years old that anyone much heard of Torquemada. But he had just been waiting in the wings of history. When Isabella became Queen of Castile, Torquemada became her chaplain. From that day on he nagged at her to let him start the Inquisition until she said O.K. Her natural choice to head the Holy Office was Tomás de Torquemada.

Now he was ready for his great lifework. There was a problem, though, Spain was about the best Roman Catholic country you could find, being loyal to the Christian Corporation, believing even the most outlandish of Catholic doctrine, and sending bags of money to the pope by every mail. Heretics were hard to come by in the Spain of Torquemada's day, and without heretics to burn you just can't have a proper Inquisition. Now here is where we see Torquemada's resourcefulness. He announced that since Christian heretics were in short supply, the Inquisition would go after the Jews.

Spain, at this time, was full of Jews, although after Torquemada completed his contribution to the Christian Corporation, there wasn't a Jew to be found in the country. But up until this time the average Spaniard had been completely unaware of the menace to the purity of the faith posed by the Jews. They got along fine with their Jewish neighbors. They married them. Many Jews had converted to Christianity, and were as orthodox as anybody.

But when you need an easily identifiable minority to persecute, Jews are always an excellent choice. They have been a favorite target of despots, dictators, and inquisitors of one kind and another down through history, so we can only admire Torquemada's sagacity in choosing them. After all, Jews have an unhappy habit of working harder, being smarter, and getting richer than their Christian neighbors, and it is always easy for people to hate the rich, the diligent, and the talented. All you have to do is to point out to people that the Jews are better off than they are and you have no trouble at all getting a pogrom going. This is what Torquemada did.

A SINCERE PERSECUTOR OF THE JEWS

We do not want to be unfair to Torquemada and lead you to believe that he was insincere in his hatred of the Jews, that it was only a cynical political strategy to insure the success of the Inquisition. Torquemada was not that kind of man, a moral mountebank, a calculating political opportunist. He had spiritual integrity. He really hated Jews. Some people insist that he only pretended to hate the Jews because it is a well-established fact that he was partly Jewish, but psychologists have explained this to our satisfaction, although we don't want to go into that here.

At any rate, Torquemada's record for persecuting Jews is impressive by any measurement. In a few short years the Holy Office burned between two and three thousand Jews, and imprisoned about a hundred thousand. We know these are insignificant figures compared, say, to what we are able to accomplish today. But Torquemada did not have fire bombs or napalm. Nor did he go in for burning whole villages. He did not burn a heretic until the heretic was duly convicted, either through trial or torture, and then he burned them one at a time. Nonetheless, taking into consideration the limitations within which he had to work, he must be judged as most efficient.

Finally, Torquemada got a law passed which expelled all Jews from Spain, and the great days of the Spanish Inquisition were over. Torquemada retired to a monastery and spent his declining years in prayer and pious contemplation. We are assured by his biographers, who would have no reason to lie to us, that he was a pleasant, soft-spoken man who was often compared to Christ by his contemporaries.

A DEFENSE OF THE INQUISITION

The Holy Office, especially the Spanish Inquisition, has received mixed reviews from historians. Sabatini speaks of it as an "engine of destruction whose wheels drip the blood of mangled generations." Doctor Rule verges on intemperance in his condemnation of it as bestial in its savagery, a blot on the escutcheon of the Christian Corporation, and a work of sadism seldom matched in mankind's weary history. Some attribute the Spanish horrors to Torquemada's unhealthy sexual repressions, but we think this is being pretty nasty, and anyway, how would they know? Garcia Rodrigo, on the other hand, lauds its work of purification, credits it with the production of all sorts of spiritual graces, religious virtues, and desirable political results, and laments that we do not have it yet with us to shape up a world which has degenerated into a shambles of liberal and permissive ways of thinking.

Mario Puzo, not exactly a historian, but possessed of a scholar's grasp of the Sicilian Mafia, attributes the origin and rise of the Mafia to the Inquisition. He says, in his novel *The Godfather,* that Sicily was a land "cruelly raped" by the Inquisition, which had "tortured rich and poor alike." The Church, he says, "exercised absolute power," and the police were the instruments of its power. The Mafia was organized as an outlaw force to combat what these Sicilian peasants viewed as an unjust, repressive, vicious, rapacious religious institution.

While we feel that Mr. Puzo is unnecessarily harsh in his description of the Inquisition's activities, his account bolsters our contention that, overall, the Inquisition was a beneficent influence. These Sicilian peasants were good folk, no doubt, but they were ignorant and unable to understand that the Holy Office had their spiritual welfare as its only motive. By willful resistance to the legitimate power and authority of the Christian Corporation (much as student protestors, peaceniks, and the like resist legitimate political authority today), they let loose the Mafia upon the world, and you know what a nuisance it is. Mr. Puzo is inclined to blame the Inquisition for the Mafia, but we think the correct view is that the Sicilian peasantry and its refusal to submit to the benevolent, if firm, rule of the Christian Corporation is the real culprit.

THE PROTESTANTS IMITATE THE INQUISITION

We must not leave the impression that inquisitional procedures were exclusively practiced by the Roman Catholic branch of the Christian Corporation. When the Holy Office got started there wasn't any corporation other than Romanism, of course. But you can't prevent imitation of a good thing. When Protestantism got going, it attempted to develop its own brand of thought control and repressive measures against heretics. We shall see, shortly, that John Calvin, the great Reformation leader at Geneva, was fond of burning heretics, although his accomplishments fall far short of Torquemada's. John Knox had a taste for violence and bloodshed. And what the orthodox Protestants did to the Roman Catholics in England during Elizabeth's rule is a caution.

But historian W. E. H. Lecky points out that the Protestants never really got the hang of persecution. He does not reproach the Protestants for lack of zeal in harassing heretics, but lays their lack of success to faulty organization. The Church of Rome, he says, "persecuted to the full extent of the power of her clergy, and that power was very great. The persecution of which every Protestant church was guilty was measured by the same rule, but clerical influence in Protestant countries was comparatively weak."

It is not for us to say whether it would be a good thing or a bad thing for the modern Christian Corporation to resort to inquisitional methods today to shore up the sagging walls of faith. We do not dispute the oft-heard contention that among leaders of the modern Christian Corporation there is many a man with the instincts of a Torquemada, and that given the same opportunity they could acquit themselves fully as well as the great Spaniard.

THE SECULAR WORLD COPIES THE INQUISITION

But that opportunity will not come. Heresy has moved from the theological and religious sphere to the political. It is now the government rather than the Church which demands loyalty oaths on threat of painful reprisals. Today it is the shadowy espionage agencies which are proficient at refined forms of torture rather than the solemn clerics of the Holy Office. Violence and murder are presently the hallmarks of the Ku Klux Klan, the Black Panthers, and the Students for a Democratic Society, instead of Inquisitors of the Faith. The pastor of any middle-class parish of the modern Christian Corporation need fear no retribution should he choose to attack orthodox theological dogma, but knows he risks excommunication if he questions orthodox political and economic dogma.

Whatever our evaluation of the Holy Office, though, the least we can say about it is that it did the job it was designed to do, which was to suppress independent thinking, inspire loyalty to the Church, and build the dikes higher against the rising tide of rebellious spirits who would have fractured the Christian Corporation centuries earlier than they did had it not been for the Inquisition. It served the Christian Corporation well in its hour of need. Let us remember it for that.

XV. *Martin Luther disjoints the Christian Corporation—a melancholy tale*

We come now to the cheerless chronicle of the Protestant Reformation. Having just beheld the beauty and perfection of the medieval church, universally acknowledged to have been the high-water mark of the Christian Corporation, the story of the Reformation, we fear, is liable to induce in us a state of melancholy.

We do not need to tell you that the culprit in this case is Martin Luther and it makes it all the worse that he started out as a good guy. He was a loyal son of the Christian Corporation, obedient to duly constituted ecclesiastical authority, unquestioning, uncritical of even the batty doctrines essential to faith and order. What makes him doubly reprehensible to all sensitive and knowledgeable men is that he was an Augustinian monk, an employee of the Christian Corporation whose unity he wrecked. It was true then, as it is true now, that when a corporation buys you and pays for you, you owe it a mindless loyalty. This, Luther, to his eternal shame, did not render.

To understand Luther—and we must try to understand him—it is necessary to recall the lovely, monolithic façade of faith erected and sturdily mortised into the medieval social system by the Christian Corporation.

Basic to this structure of faith was the assumption that God wants you to be good, but that you want to be bad—a proposition entirely consistent with the facts. From long experience in observing human frailty the Church said you can divide sins into two classes. Most horrible are those sins that are a sure ticket to hell—pride, greed, sloth, gluttony, anger, envy and despair.[1] On the other hand, such lapses as lying, cheating on your income tax, missing church services and the like are sins all right, but they do not have nearly so much damnation power as the deadly sins.

The second assumption of the medieval Church is that, though you need to be free of all the sins, and full of the seven cardinal virtues to get into heaven, it just isn't reasonable to expect you to accomplish it on your own—another assumption which appears to be free of faulty logic.

THE PENITENTIAL SYSTEM MADE CLEAR

Fortunately for you, the medieval Church said, God has entrusted to the care of the Christian Corporation[2] the responsibility for keeping you out of hell. It is able to do this because, through its hierarchy of priests, bishops, archbishops, on up to the pope, it has the power to forgive sins. No other institution could make this claim.

The Church had two aims so far as your sinning was concerned. It aimed to forgive your past sins, and it aimed to help you stay away from sinning in the future—although it was considerably more optimistic about its ability to forgive past sins than it was about its ability to prevent future sinning. It did its forgiving through the seven sacraments, which could be administered only by an ordained official of the Christian Corporation.

It was a neat system. The great charm of the medieval Church's penitential procedure was precision. Sins were precisely measured. What you had to do to be forgiven was precisely calculated. And

---

[1] These, of course, are the seven deadly sins. For some reason the medieval Church loved the number seven. The seven deadly sins had as opposites the seven cardinal virtues. There were also seven works of mercy and seven sacraments. We do not doubt that the number seven has a peculiar spiritual significance, but we are not told what it is.

[2] Roman branch.

once you had filled the prescription, you had the peace of mind enjoyed only by those who have squared things with the Almighty.

We might wonder why everyone docilely accepted the penitential system, because, admittedly, the claim that one institution could dole out spiritual reprieves just because it said it could seems a little flimsy. The reason was that back then everyone was mortally afraid of going to hell, and very much wanted to believe that someone or something could provide fire insurance.

The Christian Corporation was only doing what any alert business would do in similar circumstances—it marketed a commodity (salvation) for which there was great demand. The Church has always known that it is unnecessary to document your claims for your product when the public's desire to enjoy its blessings is very strong. Does Halo prove that its hair rinse will turn a mousey female into an instant sex symbol? Does Brylcream submit us evidence that its hair goo can rescue any clod from social oblivion? Of course not. It would be expensive to do so, maybe impossible, and is not at all necessary. All successful business enterprises understand that when you assure people that your product will fulfill one of their powerful emotional needs, you move the merchandise. This is why the modern advertising industry has been such a benison to mankind. This is also why the Christian Corporation has had no difficulty, over the centuries, peddling unexaminable theologies and undemonstrable propositions such as the penitential system.

Also essential to the medieval penitential system was the Church's teaching that on the judgment day all the dead would be raised up and then would have to submit to the verdict of the celestial courts. There were even pictures in churches of the dead getting up on judgment day and getting dressed to appear in court. They do not look very cheerful. When your case came up, there would be three possibilities. You could be sent to hell. This was an eternal sentence with no reprieve. It was described as a pretty bad place, so it was worth some repenting and even refraining from your favorite sins more often than you liked in order to escape it.

At the other extreme was heaven, a state of eternal bliss. But not many people counted on qualifying for heaven right off the bat. That left purgatory. Purgatory was for people who hadn't died in a state of being unforgiven, and whose sins were scarcely severe enough to deserve a sentence to hell, but who needed some shaping up before they were acceptable to the society of paradise.

Purgatory can best be described as a supernatural reform school where you are punished for your misdemeanors. It is not a desirable place to spend much time, and everyone who is there is terribly anxious to get out and go on to heaven.

The doctrine of purgatory is the key to the medieval penitential system. If you were in hell, the Church couldn't do anything for you. If you were in heaven, you didn't need anything done for you. But if you were in purgatory, you not only needed help, but it was readily available. By saying special masses for your soul the Church could shorten your sojourn in purgatory, even by several million years. The only catch was that you can't expect a priest to mumble all that Latin for nothing, so it was essential to leave a little something in your will to provide for the masses, or at least have relatives to pick up the tab. Pricing and product guarantee were, naturally, the province of the Christian Corporation.

LUTHER'S FASCINATION WITH SIN

It was the penitential system that Martin Luther attacked. This is very strange, because no one was more fascinated by sin and forgiveness than Luther. One reason he gave up a career at law and became an Augustinian monk was that he believed it would be much easier to save his soul as a monk than as a lawyer, an entirely rational conclusion we would think. He fasted, prayed and confessed so much that he scarcely had time or strength to commit any sins to fast and pray about and confess.[3]

Luther still felt awfully sinful, and as a last resort began rummaging around in the Bible for help.[4] He came across some pas-

[3] His confessor, Johann Von Staupitz, told Luther he was bored as hell with all the trivial sins Luther was confessing. He advised Luther to commit some higher-class sins or he wasn't going to listen to him any more.
[4] In those days the Church discouraged its constituents from reading the Bible. This is understandable, inasmuch as the Bible contains much racy material, fully as sexy as the works of Jaqueline Susann, only better written. Luther, though, as an accredited official of the Corporation, had full access to the Scriptures.

sages in the letters of Paul which advanced the idea that you cannot and do not have to earn your salvation by repenting and doing good works. All you have to do, Paul said, is to trust in the goodness and love of God. At this time Luther, still a monk, was also professor at the new university at Wittenberg, which is in what is now Germany, and pastor of the local church as well. Before long he was lacing his sermons with the doctrine of salvation by faith alone instead of by penance and good works—without any visible effects, we have to report.[5]

Probably no more would have come of it than comes of most doctrinal preaching, except that Luther's discovery of salvation by faith coincided with a papal campaign to sell indulgences. Indulgences, to describe them simply, are passes out of purgatory. You pay your money, then the Corporation certifies that your sins (or the sins of someone already in purgatory—the choice is the payer's) are remitted and you don't have to stay in purgatory, at least not very long.

A monk named Tetzel was made what we would today refer to as the sales manager for the campaign. Now we must remember that the pope, who was Leo X, and by all recognized as not the best chairman of the board ever to grace the Christian Corporation,[6] was selling indulgences for the most laudable of reasons—the building of St. Peter's at the Vatican. The trouble started when some of Luther's Wittenberg parishioners bought indulgences from Tetzel, then demanded that Luther, as their pastor, honor them. Luther replied that they weren't any good, or at least weren't necessary, as salvation was a gift of God.

We can immediately see that if the product which the Church was selling was now to be given away, the whole structure of medieval Christendom was threatened. It was a situation comparable to if, say, our federal government, in its benevolence, suddenly announced that henceforth life insurance would be given to every

[5] A congregation pays attention to what a pastor says in his sermons in inverse proportion to how well they know and like him. The people at Castle Church, Wittenberg, liked Luther. They listened respectfully to his preaching of this new doctrine and said to one another, "Well, old Martin is spouting those nutty ideas of his again."

[6] He liked hunting, carnivals, and spending money right and left better than he liked praying.

citizen without cost. What would happen to Prudential? How long would Metropolitan last?

THE NINETY-FIVE THESES DO THEIR DIRTY WORK

Tetzel and his indulgence merchants complained to the pope that Luther was hurting business in Germany. Still nothing happened. Then Luther, who—jolly chap that he was—became irritated rather easily, wrote down some nasty things about the practice of selling indulgences, along with some other intemperate criticisms of the Christian Corporation, and nailed them to the door of his church. All he meant by this was a challenge to debate his point of view, a common custom in those days. So far as the history of the Protestant schism goes, though, this was the moment when the egg hit the fan. Since Luther had ninety-five propositions in his challenge to debate, this document has become famous as "The Ninety-Five Theses." The date when he nailed it to the church door was October 31, 1517, which is the date historians accept as the sundering of the Christian Corporation into a Catholic Corporation and a Protestant Corporation, although the division took many years to accomplish.

The Corporation did everything a reasonable man could expect of it in an attempt to heal the breech. First, it tried to bribe Luther into shutting up by the promise of a cardinal's hat.

Becoming a cardinal is nothing to sneeze at if you are a poor Augustinian monk, but Luther was having too much fun leading a revolution. Then it tried to bust him by excommunicating him and warning him that he had better stay out of dark alleys. But he just went into hiding for two years and translated the New Testament into German. The only conclusion we can reach is that Luther was incorrigible.

Luther spent the rest of his life organizing and leading his schismatic church in Germany. But we give him too much credit if we award the spectacular success of his movement to personal charisma. Much of what he accomplished is attributable to his brazen exploitation of the meaner human motives.

For example, he published a little tract entitled *On Good Works*. In it he adumbrated the preposterous notion that any kind of worthwhile daily employment, from milking a cow to sweeping a room, is just as sacred as praying in church and giving tithes to the Church. This was another serious challenge to the medieval Christian Corporation. Indeed, "praying and paying" were basic to its operation. It had made praying and paying inseparable.[7] The people, of course, liked Luther's idea. While they didn't object to praying, they weren't as keen on it as the Church said they ought to be. They weren't keen on paying at all. So by appealing to the miserliness and greed of the people, Luther sought to further his so-called spiritual crusade.

The appeal to personal greed worked so well that the Reformation went national with it. By splitting off from Rome, the Church in Germany no longer needed to send money to the Vatican. Quite naturally, the kings and princes and politicians of Germany found this irresistibly alluring. They could now pocket the prodigious amounts which formerly had gone to Corporation headquarters. Best of all, they could exercise their cupidity in the name of piety—and no politician will pass up an opportunity like that.

LUTHER FAILS TO MAKE ANY IMPORTANT MONEY OUT OF THE REFORMATION

We are willing to admit that Luther, personally, was a pleasant enough chap. Though subject to fits of melancholy, and always being hounded by the devil, he was much in demand as a drinking companion. He wrote well and voluminously. Katherine Von Bora, a nun whom he married to show the pope he didn't believe in the celibacy of the clergy, found him an excellent husband in every respect, except maybe as a provider. Luther never had the ability to feather his own nest financially on the scale we would expect of a man of his acumen and opportunities. This is ironic, because the Protestant Ethic—which grew out of Luthern theology and is so largely responsible for the prosperity of the American middle class—

---

[7] Except in cases where it was very inconvenient or annoying for you to pray, the Corporation permitted you to pay more and pray less.

holds that you can tell how well God likes you by the size of your bank account. Or to put it another way, your credit rating in heaven is exactly the same as your credit rating on earth.

We must confess that Luther, at the start, had no thought of splitting the Christian Corporation. He only wanted to reform it. Nor would we hide from our readers' eyes that here and there were a few defects in the Corporation which might have been improved a little. Perhaps it had been unnecessary to burn John Huss, a reforming predecessor of Luther's. Maybe the going price for bishoprics was excessively high. For the pope and bishops to keep mistresses if they chose was accepted practice, and who can be censorius since it helped preserve the principle of the celibacy of the clergy. But they could have been more discreet about it. However, even in the best-run corporations minor irregularities will appear from time to time. So we feel that Luther made a mountain out of a molehill. Then, when the Christian Corporation fired him for cause he started his own corporation, discarding such time-honored theologies as the Mass always in Latin, the rule that said one could contact God only through a priest, the celibacy of the clergy, the financial support of the Vatican, and many more bulwarks of Corporation procedure. Disloyalty indeed!

Let us, though, drape the mantle of charity over Luther's revolt. There is no getting around the fact that, from the standpoint of the continuing unity of the Christian Corporation, he is a villain of the blackest hue. After Luther, never again was Western Christendom to exhibit that unshattered grandeur undentable by the puny attacks of its enemies, which we find so awesome today in General Motors Corporation or The National Rifle Association. But what is done is done. In the four and a half centuries since Luther the Protestant divisions of the Christian Corporation, added together, make a sizable religious establishment. It may not be good, but it is big, and bigness always must be reckoned with.

XVI. *Calvin and Knox construct Presbyterianism*

If you are a loyal product of the Protestant division of the Christian Corporation, you no doubt look to John Calvin rather than Martin Luther as your inspiration. John Calvin, more nearly than any other person, embodies in his life and personality those habits and values and stance toward the world which Protestant Christians view as ideal.

Once Luther had opened the floodgates of reform, other malcontents were sure to swim through. One of these was John Calvin. He was a Frenchman, which we suppose excuses a lot. He became a follower of Protestantism and managed to set himself up as the director of a project to turn Geneva, Switzerland, from a Catholic town into a Protestant town.

As dictator of Geneva, Calvin made everybody toe the line in religion, political thinking, and personal habits, because he was so opposed to the oppressive ideas and practices of the Roman Church, and he didn't want any of those things creeping into his city. Unlike Luther, who—after he got over worrying about his soul—enjoyed fully the pleasures of the present world, Calvin didn't get any special fun out of eating and drinking and sex. It was his conviction that no one else ought to get any special fun out of eating, drinking and sex, either, so the religious teachings and public laws of Geneva were designed to encourage you to keep all these activities at a minimum, and to make you feel guilty even for that. Calvin was also adamant about the necessity for everyone being theologically orthodox, although Calvin's orthodoxy was quite different from the orthodoxy of the Roman Church.[1]

CALVIN SAVES GENEVA

What Protestants like about John Calvin is the thrilling story of how he reformed Geneva. Sometimes we are given the idea that Geneva was like Newark, New Jersey, where more than the average amount of sinning goes on. It wasn't, though. A lot of sinning goes on in Newark, to be sure, but nobody there has much fun. Geneva was more like Las Vegas, also a town where more than the average amount of sinning goes on, but people have a good time at it.

Calvin soon put a stop to the sinning. The Genevese were reluctant to abandon their lax moral habits, but Calvin showed them that it was best that they do so. The way he showed them was by imprisoning, hanging, or burning anyone who did not abandon his lax moral habits. Since people often become addicted to fleshly pleasures, Calvin helped them break their bad habits by closing the taverns, cleaning up the red-light district, and strictly enforcing the law that everyone had to attend church every Sunday and "listen to the sermon devoutly."

We cannot withhold our approval from the fruits of Calvin's reforming endeavors in Geneva. What he accomplished was the demonstration of an entirely new concept of the relationship between the political corporation and the Christian Corporation. Recall that we mentioned in an earlier chapter that the Christian Corporation developed the theory of the Christian Corporation looking after the spiritual side of man's nature, and the political corporation looking after the earthly or material side of man's nature. The relationship here is one of co-operation. Calvin's idea was to merge the two

[1] We mustn't forget that whether you are orthodox or not depends on who is defining orthodoxy. At the Vatican, the pope defined it and said Calvin was unorthodox. In Geneva, Calvin defined it and said the pope was unorthodox. Theologians, though no two of them ever agree as to what constitutes orthodoxy, are always very certain of what it is, but laymen often have to step lively to be sure they aren't standing on heretical ground.

corporations with the Christian part of the merger controlling everything in sight. The technical name for such an arrangement is "theocracy." Protestants, since Calvin, have looked on the theocratic organization of society, so long as it is a Protestant theocracy, as the ideal toward which mankind should move. Prohibition, Sunday blue laws, censorship of stage and screen, anti-smut campaigns—all these are manifestations of the theocratic impulse. Since Calvin, the Roman Catholics have had theocratic impulses, too, but prefer a Roman Catholic theocracy with Roman Catholic rules on birth control and freedom of the press and other such things binding on everyone. The theocratic ideal never caught on, though, and today Geneva is no better and no worse than any other middle-size city.

PREDESTINATION EXPLAINED

John Calvin did leave one enduring monument. That is *The Institutes of the Christian Religion,* the definitive work on Protestant theology. Although Calvin filled up fifty-nine quarto volumes writing it, we can sum it up as follows: God doesn't like everybody. Those He likes He causes to prosper on earth, and for them reserves a good address in heaven. Those He doesn't like face a cheerless existence here and bleak prospects hereafter. This is known as "predestination." The doctrine of predestation is more popular among the prosperous than it is among the poor. No one denies, though, that Calvin's theology is one of the sturdier beams in the framework of the Protestant Reformation, and an indispensable source of intellectual inspiration for the Protestant Christian Corporation today, especially since their corporation specializes in ministering to the prosperous.

KNOX SAVES SCOTLAND

Nor must we forget John Calvin's contribution toward the reforming of Scotland. He didn't do it himself, being far too busy reforming

Geneva to get away. It was done by one of Calvin's pupils and most ardent admirers, John Knox.

We all recall how Mary, Queen of Scots, made life quite unpleasant for any Scotsmen of the Protestant persuasion. This is why John Knox accepted the post of pastor of the English-speaking church in Geneva. It was in Geneva, under Calvin's tutelage, that he learned how to establish a truly Christian, democratic theocracy. When a sufficient number of Scottish nobles got fed up with Mary and her allegiance to repressive Roman Church practices, they invited Knox to come back to Scotland to "establish the most blessed word of God and His congregation." Historians tell us that these Scottish nobles were more interested in their own secular power than they were in reforming Scotland, but we find this hard to believe in the light of the pious and Godly language in which they stated their purpose.

John Knox, as a good student of Calvin's, was—like Calvin—most heartily opposed to any system of church government which had bishops, because bishops have the power to oversee parishes, and recommend to the congregations who shall be their pastor, and control finances. So when he established the Church of Scotland he abolished the hateful and dictatorial office of bishop. Under his plan of reform, the Church of Scotland had "superintendents," who had the power to oversee parishes and recommend to the congregations who shall be their pastor, and control finances. It was apparent to all that this was a victory of democratic church government over autocratic episcopal church government.

Many Scotsmen, though, remained perversely loyal to the old, oppressive Roman branch of the Christian Corporation. To enable them to see how much more benevolent and free was the new Scotch brand of Christianity, John Knox was forced to pass a law that you would be executed for going to Mass. However, the death penalty only applied when you were caught at Mass the third time, which seems to us most reasonable and merciful.

Many disgruntled people accused Knox of being a sort of Presbyterian pope, claiming that he actually ran everything in the Church of Scotland to suit himself. This is terribly unfair. He never even held the post of "superintendent." He was only pastor of St.

Giles Church in Edinburgh. Being pastor of St. Giles Church in Edinburgh was (and still is) the most important and prestigious job in the Church of Scotland, but we feel certain it was only a coincidence that John Knox was selected for it.

To carry out the reformation of the Christian Corporation in Scotland the bad old creeds of Romanism, which you formerly had to promise to believe, were thrown away. In their place was put a good new Calvinistic creed or confession of faith which you had to promise to believe. This creed was written by John Knox.

Also, the bad old Roman plan of church organization with parishes organized into dioceses under bishops was discarded. Instead, the Church of Scotland adopted a good new plan of organization with parishes organized into synods and presbyteries, and, as we have mentioned, superintendents administering them instead of bishops. This plan of organization was drawn up by John Knox.

When you have a reformation it is absolutely necessary to discard the liturgies and worship practices of the Church you are reforming. The Church of Scotland abolished the old Roman rites and substituted *The Book of Common Order,* which contained new liturgies and rules for worship. *The Book of Common Order* was written by John Knox.

John Knox was every bit as successful in reforming Scotland as John Calvin was successful in reforming Geneva. Their importance for us today rests on the fact that Calvin and Knox invented the form of church government known as Presbyterianism, and we all know how successful Presbyterianism has become in the American branch of the Christian Corporation. Presbyterianism to this day is characterized by the free and democratic spirit in church government, following the precedent set by Calvin and Knox. It is also characterized by an intense loyalty to predestination theology (which we explained to you earlier in the chapter) following the precedent established by Calvin and Knox. You would have to look awfully hard to find two men who, as a team, have done more for the Christian Corporation than John Calvin and John Knox.

REFORMERS TRY TO REFORM THE REFORMERS

One of the problems you run into when you start a reformation directed against the establishment is that before long your reformation is also an establishment, and then some of your followers of the more volatile type try to reform you. History shows us that no reformers ever enjoyed being reformed by other reformers.

John Calvin in particular suffered terribly from people who sought to correct him and his reformation.

There was a Genevese pastor named Caroli who tried to reform Calvin by saying publicly that Calvin was not entirely orthodox in his theological views. Nothing much came of it though, because, by coincidence we are sure, shortly after Caroli made his charges he was encouraged to leave the profession of the ministry. We are told that he could have refused to leave, but that some kind and helpful people pointed out to him that the alternatives to leaving were not attractive, so he left.

Then there was a doctor by the name of Jerome Hermes Bolsec who went around saying that Calvin was wrong about the doctrine of predestination and that it just wasn't so. Such scurrilous talk as this was not to be tolerated, of course, and Calvin was forced to banish Bolsec from Geneva. However, Bolsec went somewhere else and published what we are told was a "grossly slanderous" biography of Calvin, which wasn't very nice of Bolsec, although ex-White House aids and former secretaries to people like Jackie Kennedy Onassis do the same thing today to the increase of their own fame and fortune.

Then there was Michael, or Miguel, Servetus, another doctor, who wrote many derogatory articles on such established Christian doctrines as the Nicene explanation of the Holy Trinity, Chalcedonian Christology, infant baptism, and the infallibility of John Calvin. Since it would have been most damaging to the Christian Corporation in Geneva to have another doctor writing a slanderous biography of John Calvin it was decided that the best thing for all concerned was to burn Doctor Servetus at the stake. While we may feel that such measures border on the severe, we also realize that it is necessary to be firm in defense of the faith, and agree that Calvin had little choice but to make a bonfire out of the misguided, heretical Doctor Servetus.

All this goes to show us that life for reformers such as John Calvin is never easy, and the trials and tribulations they have to endure for the sake of the Christian Corporation are harrowing indeed. We feel certain, though, that they were glad to endure them for the sake of the Pearly Gates Syndicate.

XVII. *Ignatius Loyola and the Counter-Reformation—or the Christian Corporation strikes Back*

It is an axiom of organizational control that once the virus of revolt lays hold, the disease will rampage throughout the entire body of the corporation. That is exactly what happened after Lutheranism infected the Christian Corporation.

Who would have dreamed, for example, that a staunch son of the Church such as Henry VIII of England would have caught the Protestant bacteria? He had been the most loyal of the loyal to the pope. Leo X had conferred on him the rarely bestowed title "Defender of The Faith."[1] But Henry set up the Church of England as a national church and named himself the head of the church. Thus, the Reformation came to England, although it was never a part of Luther's movement because Henry didn't like Lutherans.

REFORMATIONS EVERYWHERE

Before long, reformations were going on everywhere. We have seen how John Calvin reformed Geneva. Then there was John Knox reforming Scotland, and William of Orange reforming the Netherlands, and King Christian III reforming Scandinavia, or parts of it.

---

[1] The title was granted in appreciation for Henry's book against Luther. The pope didn't actually read the book, and neither did many other people, but it was reputed to have had a magnificent binding.

It would be profitless for us to examine these reformations in detail, because they all follow the same dreary pattern, which is to abolish one Christian Corporation and set up another one in its place.

The Roman branch of the Christian Corporation, which, as we know, in those days was the true Christian Corporation, didn't take all this subversive activity lying down. Under Pope Paul III it launched a movement known in history as the Counter-Reformation.

The hero of the Counter-Reformation was a Spaniard named Ignatius Loyola. He started life as a soldier, but was severely wounded and had to give up a military career. During his recovery he decided that what the Christian Corporation needed was a band of Christian soldiers with spiritual muscles hard as rocks, ready and willing to do anything whatever for the good of the cause. The purpose of his little army of Christ was to mount search-and-destroy missions against heretics, schismatics, and other undesirables, and then carry out pacification programs to secure enemy country for the Christian Corporation. This order was called the Society of Jesus, or the Jesuits. It was comparable to our marines. It would go anywhere and do anything to clean up messy situations for the Church.

Loyola was a superb executive, an organizational genius of the highest caliber. For people like Loyola, Wall Street or Madison Avenue gladly pay well up in six figures, plus a plethora of fringe benefits including stock options, private jets, and hunting lodges in the Adirondacks.

CHRISTIAN CONDITIONING

Anyone who became a Jesuit was processed by a rigorous period of training. He first took vows of poverty, chastity, and absolute obedience not only to the pope but to the head of the Jesuits, who —carrying out the military pattern of the order—was called the general. The society selected the general, except Loyola selected the first general of the society.[2]

Next, a member was conditioned by a course in *The Spiritual*

2 He selected himself.

Exercises. The Spiritual Exercises is a training manual, written by Loyola. According to the manual, the candidate for membership had to be brainwashed of all his former values, such as pleasure, love of family, etc., and taught to put the good of the order above every other value in life, even be willing to suffer and die for it. This, we see immediately, is a scheme of values not too different than that preached by the modern business corporation, although the modern corporation is more subtle about it.

Like the Jesuits, the modern business corporation describes for you the bliss which awaits the corporate executive who is willing to work long hours, skimp on family life, give up friends who would be a handicap to his career, and conform rigidly to the corporation's concept of the corporate executive. Unlike the Jesuits, though, who flatly stated that you might get killed in the line of duty, the modern corporation neglects to tell you that the price of executive success may be hypertension, heart attack, high cholesterol, or a perforated ulcer. It doesn't even warn you that cirrhosis of the liver is a likely result of the four-martini business lunch.

After a candidate was properly brainwashed he was indoctrinated with the ethical concepts of "probabilism" and "intentionalism." We will attempt to explain probabilism and intentionalism, although they are a little intricate.

Probabilism says that before you do something you have to be able to imagine that the results of what you are going to do could be good results, however remote the actual possibility of the results being good. An example of probabilism would be that you should seduce a girl—though seduction, of course, is technically a sin— if you think it probable that the results will be that she will feel remorse for her wicked ways and rectify her life. The point is that remorse for sin is a good result, so the seduction is a good thing to do, although without the ethical concept of probablism as your motive, seduction is a very bad thing to do.

Intentionalism is not too different from probabilism. What it means is that the goodness or badness of any act can be located in the intent or purpose of the person doing the act. Let us say that your intention is to save someone from going to hell for the sin of heresy. It is generally agreed that heresy is one of the sins most offensive to God. It is, therefore, a good intent to save the heretic, even if he is recalcitrant and you have to use the rack and the thumb-screw, or confiscate all his property, or in extreme cases hang or burn him. Any of these measures would be construed as undesirable if your intent was just to vent some of your kinky ideas, or to enrich yourself. But these acts take on an entirely different com-plexion when it is clear that your intent is for the poor guy's own good.

THE ETHICAL FLEXIBILITY OF PROBABILISM AND INTENTIONALISM

As we can readily see, an ethical perspective based on probabilism and intentionalism allows considerably more flexibility of action than conventional codes of Christian conduct which spell out in detail what you can and can't do.[3]

The Jesuit program to abort the Protestant Reformation was based on three thrusts of faith: (1) preaching to convert non-Romans and to correct heretics; (2) provide plenty of opportunity for confession; (3) establish schools everywhere to disseminate right ideas. The Jesuits were glad to convert and confess anyone, but as one his-torian puts it, "their excellent schools were not for the multitude, but for the wellborn and well to do." This may offend our demo-cratic sensibilities, but history demonstrates that the multitudes usually ape the styles and habits of the privileged, so if you can keep the privileged loyal to the Christian Corporation it is likely that the multitudes will remain loyal also.

The Jesuits, as you would expect from this brief description of their methods, were a thumping success. They stemmed the on-rushing tide of the Protestant Reformation. Some of the measures they had to take it is better we don't tell you about. Even the Vatican found them objectionable, and back then, we regret to say, the Vatican was fairly permissive about what you had to do to keep the faithful in line. For a brief period the pope banned the Society

[3] Conventional Christians who believe you have to stick to the rules do not necessarily behave any better than Christian probabilists and intentionalists, but they often feel guilty. Christian probabilists and intentionalists, on the other hand, need never be troubled by guilt feelings.

of Jesus. The ban was soon lifted, though, because this kind of ruthless, efficient employees are hard for a corporation to come by. Today The Society of Jesus is in perfectly good odor with the Roman Catholic branch of the modern Christian Corporation, although we expect it has modified some of its methods.

We also have to mention another strategy of the counter-Reformation. This was the Council of Trent, which met from 1545 to 1563.[4] We mention it because the Council of Trent was the council which agreed on an unalterable, unchangeable definition of Roman-brand Christianity which would stand forever. This definition said that all authority in the Christian Corporation, Roman branch, resides in the pope and the *Curia.* It fixed clerical celibacy as absolutely binding forever, a subject which, henceforth, would not even be debatable. We know, of course, that since Vatican I and Vatican II there has been some little discussion about the absolute power of the pope and the Curia, and even a voice raised here and there questioning the wisdom of clerical celibacy. But the present pope is defending stoutly against any attempts at reform. In the light of what the Council of Trent said about a medieval Catholicism being the unchangeable description of Catholicism, we don't see how he could take any other position, so we doubt that much will come of these clamorings for change in the Roman Church.

THE END OF THE MONOLITHIC CHRISTIAN CORPORATION

As a result of the Protestant Reformation and the Catholic counter-Reformation, the idea of one Christian Corporation dominating the Western world was reduced to a pile of shards and unrepairable. What you had was two leading brands of Christianity—Romanism, which was under the pope, and Protestantism, which, though strong and healthy by now, was split up into numberless national churches, factions, sects, groups, theologies, etc.

[4] The pope wasn't able to attend the Council often, but he sent it reams of detailed instructions as to what he expected the Council to do. Some of the Council delegates were more cynical than we think good Christians should be, and got to saying things like "The Holy Ghost just arrived from Rome in a dispatch box."

Though it started in Europe, it was in the New World that Protestantism bloomed and put forth its fairest blossoms, indeed became the dominant Christian Corporation. We shall now turn to that splendid story.

XVIII. *The Christian Corporation comes to the New World*

We now must readjust our perspectives on the Christian Corporation. Our thesis has been that unity and bigness are the watchwords for the Corporation, and we have deplored those influences—such as Luther—who have violated the unity of the Church. But one has to accept history. After the Protestant Reformation there were, in effect, not one but two Christian Corporations, both legitimate. The situation was similar to our anti-trust laws forcing Standard Oil—one big, burly corporation which could stifle all competition— to break itself up into several smaller units. These units were still big, burly corporations, but not so large or muscular as the original company had been.

What we have, then, at this point in our history, is a Roman Catholic Christian Corporation and a Protestant Christian Corporation. But as our scene of action moves to the United States we shall treat the Protestant branch as the true Christian Corporation, because in the United States it is the dominant religious organization. From now on, when we refer to the Christian Corporation without qualification we mean the Protestant Corporation.

COLUMBUS SEES TO THE CONVERSION OF THE INDIANS

The Roman branch came to the *Terra Nova,* or the new earth first, of course. Christopher Columbus, upon landing, planted the cross and the flag of Spain, then sat right down and wrote to his sponsor, His Most Catholic Majesty, King Ferdinand, that the new world was replete with commercial and missionary potential. The natives had a concept of God already, Columbus wrote, and thought that he and his men came from heaven. He saw no point in disabusing them of this notion, because it would help in processing them into Christians. Not only would conversion provide for their eternal salvation, he said, but would result in sending "much gold" home to Spain and the king.

Ferdinand, who apparently had a remarkable enthusiasm for missions, sent Columbus plenty of priests and soldiers. The priests were most successful in converting the Indians. The soldiers helped by relieving the natives of their gold, thus removing the temptation to love their money too much, because love of money is always a handicap to true spiritual insight. The soldiers employed the Indians as slaves to dig more gold, which was sent to King Ferdinand and presumably used to finance more missionary enterprises.

We are certain that, at the time, this fusion of an aggressive missionary thrust with a promising secular business appeared to be just the thing needed to win the Indians to Christianity and at the same time introduce them to the blessings of an advanced culture. But, without being critical of the good intentions of its perpetrators, we must assess the whole project as ill-conceived. We do not doubt that the natives were grateful to their conquerors for converting them and baptizing them, thus saving them from going to the bad place. Nor do we doubt that the natives also appreciated being saved from the sin of greed through Spanish appropriation of their gold. But, while producing immediate profits, the project dried up the source of the gold supply too rapidly, which is uneconomic. It was exploitation of natural resources, the kind of thing which would shock us today if our fine, large oil and coal and lumber industries indulged in it, but of course they never would.

THE PROTESTANTS STAKE OUT THEIR TERRITORIES

The various branches of the Protestant Christian Corporation also hurried to the new world and staked out sections of it for themselves.

The Puritans, who are famed for their fierce love of religious liberty, established themselves in New England. Under the Puritans, anyone living in New England was perfectly free to be a New England Puritan Congregational Christian.

The Church of England, or Episcopalians, founded Virginia. The Swedish Lutherans appropriated Delaware. Presbyterians established a religious monopoly in New Jersey and New York. Roger Williams left Massachusetts and got things started for the Baptists in Rhode Island.

No one doubts that the most glorious example of a branch of the Christian Corporation in America is the Methodist Church, or the United Methodist Church as it is now called.[1] Oddly, the Methodists—though now the single most powerful Protestant sect in America—founded no state or claimed no territory of its own in the early days of the republic. We would have thought this a poor strategy indeed, for one basic principle for capturing markets is to get in on the ground floor and establish your share of the market early.

But John Wesley, who founded Methodism in England, was an extraordinarily farsighted businessman and organizer. He trained a band of salesmen hardy enough to withstand frontier life and saturated the frontier with his brand of religion. This is why Methodism today is a national brand like Budweiser beer instead of some obscure brand sold only regionally.

We should mention, too, that the Roman Catholic branch of the Corporation established a small foothold in the United States by settling the state of Maryland. But while this sect is a large and respectable part of the Corporation today, it was not until it imported millions of members via immigration (this was in the nineteenth and twentieth centuries) that it grew much, so for our present purposes Romanism is a negligible factor.

Now you have a picture of the new Christian Corporation in America. Candor compels us to state that its beginnings were inauspicious. Every branch of the Corporation believed itself to be

[1] The Methodist Church has been acquiring, through mergers, smaller sects such as the Methodist Protestants and the Evangelical United Brethren. It is only good corporate practice that, after a number of such acquisitions, the parent company make a small change in the corporate name.

the trunk of the tree, or the one true Christian Corporation. The various denominations composing the Corporation quarreled with asperity and vigor over doctrine and church polity. It appeared that complete Christian chaos would reign forever.

What saved the situation was the heroic labors of two men— one of the eighteenth century, and one of the nineteenth. Let us look briefly at their contributions to the unity of the new Christian Corporation.

Jonathan Edwards terrorizes New England and establishes conservative Christianity in the New World

The Christian star of the eighteenth century was Jonathan Edwards. It was Edwards who, by his preaching, united the fragmented Christian Corporation. He didn't put all the various sects together in one super-organization. He did something much more effective —he forged a theology of fear which spanned sectarian differences and gathered everyone together in a band of terror.

Jonathan Edwards was born in the year 1703, the son of the Congregational pastor of East Windsor, Connecticut, which is a fairly classy place today but was then only a rough frontier village. Jonathan was the only boy in the family, but he had ten sisters. This circumstance early shaped his interest in religion. One boy among ten girls has to resort to drastic measures, so he developed the habit of indulging in extended periods of solitary meditation and prayer.

Jonathan had the first of several religious experiences when he was five or six years old. These experiences bred in him a healthy sense of personal guilt. He also developed a knack for communicating his own anxiety about his soul to others. He endeavored, he said, to spend "much time in religious conversation with other boys." To expedite these evangelical activities he persuaded a number of his little friends to help him build a shanty in a swamp so that they could have a place to which they could retire for prayer and theological discussions. Since it is a little unusual for preadolescent boys to want to go out in a swamp for lengthy private devotions, we infer that Jonathan was a persuasive speaker even at this early age.[1]

EDWARDS' WHOLESOME SENSE OF SINFULNESS

We should not look upon it as in any way unusual that Jonathan Edwards acquired early a wholesome sense of his own sinfulness. He says he was a terrible sinner at five or six, which takes us aback some, but little boys of a religious bent have always been fond of thinking of themselves as the blackest of transgressors. John Bunyan records that, as a lad, he liked to ring bells and play tipcat on Sunday, which, he said, made him "Chief of sinners." We deplore the ringing of bells and the playing of tipcat on Sunday, of course, as this is conduct which cannot be condoned. But we feel that Bunyan could not rightly lay claim to the title of chief of sinners on no better record than this, and we expect that Edwards' claim that he was a terrible evildoer was based on similar conduct. But to Edwards' credit, though he led what we would evaluate as an exemplary moral life, he never lost this oppressive awareness of the sinfulness of the human condition. His later success as a preacher is directly traceable to this prepubescent development of the ability to evoke guilty anxiety in his bearers.

At the age of thirteen Jonathan Edwards entered Yale University. We would conclude that he was a child prodigy except that this was the normal age for university matriculation in those days. Back then, when you had finished learning arithmetic, algebra, geometry, reading, writing, and one of the classical languages, there was no place else to go for further study except the university. At the university you studied arithmetic, algebra, geometry, reading, writing, and one of the classical languages.

Jonathan got along fine in his studies at the university, but he didn't get along too well with the other students. Whenever the

---

[1] Ben Franklin, a contemporary of Edwards, relates that he, too, engaged in a swamp-building project along with his little friends. But he and his playmates built, instead of a booth for prayer, a wharf for fishing—and they stole the material for building it.

students were rebelling against the college, which—we regret to say—was most of the time, Jonathan always took the side of the college authorities.

Once the students were rioting over the quality of the food the college served them, which they called pig swill and worse. But Jonathan said he liked it fine. Also, he wrote his father that the students indulged in stealing pigs and chickens, breaking windows, swearing, and "unseasonable nightwalking." He rejoiced, he said, that he was free of these "monstrous impieties and acts of immorality." Although we are inclined to be a little more tolerant of these rascally students than Edwards was, because we must recognize that not all college kids have as well-sharpened a sense of sin as Jonathan had, nonetheless his attitude is just what we ought to expect from a student preparing for the profession of the Christian ministry.[2]

After graduation, Edwards became pastor of a small Presbyterian church in New York. During this pastorate he worked out a series of thirty-four rules for the regulation of his spiritual life. Finding only thirty-four rules insufficient to cover all possible exigencies, however, he later raised the number to seventy, which strikes us as at least adequate.[3] We would recount some of these rules for you except that they are somewhat dreary, as Calvinistic principles are apt to be.

By the time he was twenty, Edwards had a thorough grasp of standard Calvinist theology. This stern Calvinism was the doctrinal stance which was to do so much for him and for the Christian Corporation. Some people have described this theological perspective which he espoused as "gloomy optimism."

GLOOMY OPTIMISM EXPLAINED

It isn't easy to explain gloomy optimism, but we must try. An example would be Edwards' teaching that we are obligated to

---

[2] Nearly all his fellow students at Yale were preparing for the Christian ministry, too.

[3] Benjamin Franklin, at about the same time, also formulated some rules for his life. But he found that thirteen rules were plenty, and admits he didn't always keep them too well.

feel terribly guilty about the pleasures of sexual intercourse in this earthly life. Hardly anyone will disagree that this is a gloomy prospect indeed. But as we are sinking into the quicksands of remorse and self-reproach, Edwards rescues us with the assertion that, on the other hand, unlimited copulation will be available to us in heaven with no guilt feelings necessary. "Every part of the saints' refined bodies shall be as full of pleasure as they can hold," he assures us, which is a powerful incentive to us to tolerate on earth all the guilt required for entry into future blessedness, and is as optimistic doctrine as you will ever find.

With the unerring judgment by which the Christian Corporation spots future leaders and elevates them early to positions of responsibility, Edwards was promoted to assistant pastor of the Congregational Church of Northampton, Massachusetts. The fact that his grandfather was the pastor of the congregation was no handicap to him in achieving this desirable appointment, we presume. Northampton was the most important town and church in the colony outside of Boston, and when his grandfather passed on two years later and Edwards became head pastor, he was in a position to begin his great work by which the world still remembers him.

This work is known to history as "The Great Awakening." What it was was a mind-blowing revival meeting which lasted several years and spread all over everywhere in New England. It was Jonathan's preaching which ignited the spiritual conflagration.

THE PROTESTANT EQUIVALENT OF PENANCE

We must pause here to explain to you the importance of preaching to the Protestant Christian Corporation. Recall that the Roman Catholic Christian Corporation featured, as its main item, forgiveness of sins and assurance of heaven through the sacraments it alone could dispense. When Luther declared the penitential system invalid it was impossible, of course, for the Protestant Corporation to do business in this tried and successful manner, so it had to find a substitute. The substitute was preaching. Instead of dispensing forgiveness by sacraments, the Protestant Corporation dispensed theology by preaching. It surprises us a little that you could build a large and powerful corporation with preaching as your main product, but you can. The casual observer tends to underestimate the market for theology. But if you are convinced that you can't get to heaven by penance, you need an alternative or you will fret all the time about your spiritual security. The only apparent alternative is salvation through correct theology, which can be purveyed effectively only by preaching.

If the new Christian Corporation had ever entertained doubts as to the efficacy of preaching, Jonathan Edwards dispelled them. He preached sermons to his Northampton congregation on such subjects as "The Justice of God in the Damnation of Sinners." It is really an excellent idea on God's part to consign you to the crackling flames of hell, he said in this sermon, because you are "a little, wretched, despicable creature; a worm, a mere nothing, and less than nothing; a vile insect, that has risen up in contempt against the Majesty of heaven and earth."

Whether this scares us or not, it petrified the town of Northampton. Nearly everyone within the city limits and many from the suburbs joined the Church in the hopes that by doing so they would at least mitigate the just but unalluring fate that surely awaited them. Everyone, that is, except Jonathan's Uncle Joseph. Uncle Joseph was so depressed over his sinful state that one Sunday morning instead of going to church he stayed home and cut his throat.

So persuasive was Edwards' preaching that it often unhinged the congregation and the people would shriek and shout and stomp around in the throes of guilt. One Sunday morning all this activity loosened the stays of the church balcony and it collapsed, dumping its contents of worshipers onto the floor of the main auditorium. Everyone thought the end of the world had come for sure, but it hadn't. No one was killed, and hardly anyone was hurt beyond barked shins and a few shiners here and there.

Edwards, who had the sure promotional instincts which would get him a fine job in advertising or TV today, immediately called a special service and preached a sermon on how the collapse of the balcony was God's warning to all the sinners in the vicinity to repent immediately. After all, he argued, you couldn't expect Jehovah to let you off this lightly the next time.

SINNERS IN THE HANDS OF AN ANGRY GOD

While this kind of preaching sparked the bonfire of the Great Awakening, the real fuel for the flames was a sermon Jonathan preached at Enfield, Connecticut in 1741. The title of the sermon was "Sinners in the Hands of an Angry God." It is perhaps the most famous sermon ever preached in America.

We would like to think that it was the impeccable logic and the inscrutable theological content of the sermon which compelled the awesome response from the congregation it received whenever and wherever it was preached, but we suspect it was the gruesome word picture he painted which did the trick. What Edwards did in the sermon was to describe how God was going to hold you dangling over the fiery pit of hell as if you were "some loathsome insect over the fire . . . ten thousand times more abominable in His eyes, than the most hateful venomous serpent is in ours . . . He will crush you under His feet without mercy; He will crush out your blood and make it fly, and it shall be sprinkled on His garments, so as to stain all His raiment."

We, of course, are accustomed to violence, and sadism, and blood all over everything, and knifings, and disembowelment, not to mention beatings and torture and other forms of brutality from watching the movies and TV. So we could take this kind of preaching in stride, and go to the kitchen for a snack, or to the bathroom, when the commercials come on if they had commercial breaks in sermons, which they sometimes do if there is a special offering to be taken. It wouldn't bother us at all.

But if you are a simple frontiersman a long way from centers of culture and sophistication, and no coaxial cable to bring culture and sophistication to you, then such preaching as this can upset you pretty fast. At least it upset the people of New England pretty fast. The Great Awakening spread over New England with the rapidity of mononucleosis at a love-in, and it can be said to have been the most vital and meaningful religious and cultural movement of the eighteenth century in America—the first half of the eighteenth century anyway.

It is difficult for a rational man to understand how a strict Calvinistic theology can produce a religious revival, especially one of the magnitude of the Great Awakening. Calvinism, you undoubtedly recall, claims that God has already selected your eternal habitat and nothing you can do will alter its site. What's the point, then, of getting saved and giving up all your interesting vices if it can't make any difference anyway? No explanation suggests itself, but for some reason which defies logic, Calvinists—who insist that good works and behaving yourself and cutting out all the sins that are so much fun won't get you anywhere with God—work harder at doing good works and behaving themselves and eliminating fun from their lives than almost any other class of sinners. There is a mystery here which sages have tried to fathom, but they can't. They always end up baffled and perplexed.

All we can say, then, is that Calvinism works, even though we don't know why it works. During the Great Awakening nearly all of New England was saved and became Christian. But after a while the juice dribbled out of the movement and New England began to get unsaved with alarming rapidity. It is discouraging to report that the congregation at Northampton got bored with Jonathan Edwards' sound, doctrinal preaching and voted to fire him after twenty-four years as their pastor.

EDWARDS ATTACKS PORNOGRAPHY AND LOSES HIS JOB

Actually, they didn't say they were bored with his preaching or that they were tired of the Great Awakening. What they said was that he wasn't good at young people's work. It seems that some of the kids in his congregation got caught passing around a dirty book. Edwards was rightly wrathful, and read from the pulpit all the names of the kids who had been boning up on sex by reading pornography. This infuriated the parents of the culprits, who said that reading pornography is the time-honored way for kids to learn about sex, saving their parents a lot of embarrassment, and so long as the John Birch Society and Billy James Hargis and that crowd won't let the public schools teach about it, how else are they going to learn?

It is pretty certain, though, that the real reason they fired him was that they were tired of the Great Awakening and all that Sinners-in-the-Hands of-an-Angry-God stuff. And while we wouldn't want to defend their callous treatment of this beloved pastor, we do admit that sustaining a Great Awakening for twenty-four years can take a lot out of you.

Edwards' career went downhill pretty fast. The only job he could find was missionary to the Indians at Stockbridge, Massachusetts, quite a comedown for the leader of the Great Awakening. We would expect that it mortified him immensely to take such a menial job, but it didn't. He was quite content with it. He was content with it because there weren't too many Indians around Stockbridge to Christianize, and he could polish off his missionary duties in a couple of hours per day, with all that time left over for writing books, which is what he really wanted to do. Perhaps the Great Awakening had exhausted him, too.

Anyway, when Princeton University offered him its presidency he was reluctant to accept, even with all the honors that went with being the head of an Ivy League school, because he knew it would take a lot more time to run a college than it did to Christianize Indians, and his writing would suffer.

He accepted, though, because few preachers can resist the proffer of a college presidency. But he wasn't president long. There was much smallpox in the Princeton area at the time, and Edwards had a famous doctor come up from Philadelphia and vaccinate him. But he must have gotten a massive or especially virulent dose of serum, because he caught the disease and died at the age of fifty-five.[4]

---

[4] As a good Calvinist, Edwards should have accepted his passing with equanimity, because all good Calvinists know that such events were foreordained before the foundation of the world. But when he learned that he had bought it, he was convinced that Providence had somehow gotten things mixed up.

CONSERVATIVE RELIGION EXPLAINED

Any assessment of Jonathan Edwards must credit him with two lasting monumental contributions to the establishment of the new American Christian Corporation.

The first contribution was philosophical. He popularized what we may loosely call "conservative religion," and made it a permanent part of our American culture. This is why Billy Graham is so welcome in the White House.

Conservative religion, in profile, focuses on the unimaginable importance of the next world and the next life as compared to the negligible significance of this world and this life. If this is true—and who can doubt that it is—then all man's earthly strivings are as fleeting as a fly on the flanks of a panther, so there is no point in trying to improve conditions here. The thing to do, according to conservative religion, is to accept with resignation your lot in this life, and run like sixty to get into heaven.

Conservative religion did so very much to win rich people to the American Christian Corporation, and thus put it on a firm financial footing. As a matter of fact, it is still winning rich people to the Corporation. Conservative religion has a special appeal to the rich, partly because it is easier for a rich man to accept with resignation his lot in this life than it is for a poor man. Also, conservative religion, with its promise of a delectable future life, helps to divert the attention of the impoverished masses from the sight of the rich man enjoying the just fruits of his labors. Churches of a conservative theological persuasion always eschew any preaching or teaching that would lead to tinkering with our proven free-enterprise economy, or encourage blacks and other lesser members of our society to material and educational aspirations for which they are obviously not ready. Privileged and worthy people appreciate this a lot, too, because it helps to stabilize society. It is hard to see how the rich could ask for more from a religion than conservative Christianity has given and is giving them. They should come

through handsomely in its financial support, and for the most part
they are very generous with conservative churches.

EDWARDS AS THE FATHER OF THE REVIVAL MEETING

Edwards' other signal contribution to the establishment of the new
American Christian Corporation was the strategy for promoting
conservative Christianity. This strategy is known as the revival
meeting. It is suspected that George Whitfield, one of John Wesley's
missionaries to America, showed Edwards how it was done. But
it was Edwards' skill in whipping a congregation into a frenzy
of fear and guilt and thus conditioning them to be easily manipulated
that pinned revivalism permanently on middle-class American culture.

The able and popular operators in the revival field today utilize
methods which would no doubt have astounded Edwards—advance
men, publicity men, accountants, financiers, satellite ventures such
as publishing houses, radio and television programming, etc., col-
lateral talent including singers, song leaders, organists, mass choirs,
stars from the world of entertainment and professional sports
coached to warm up a delighted audience, and other devices too
numerous to mention. However, all these modern refinements of
revivalism are inherent in and flow naturally from the fundamental
revivalistic strategy if not devised by, at least popularized by
Jonathan Edwards.

Jonathan Edwards, in his preaching and his efforts, demonstrated
that guilt feelings are universal, that fear of hell knows no denominational boundaries, and that both can be profitably exploited for
the building of the Christian Corporation. His was the first great
unifying voice in the sectarian wilderness of the new American
Christian Corporation, and the Corporation will ever bless him for
it.

XX. *Henry Ward Beecher introduces liberal religion to the American Christian Corporation*

We have just seen what a splendid thing was conservative Calvinistic Christianity. We now know what immeasurable good it did for people, and what a contribution Jonathan Edwards, its great advocate, made to the new American Christian Corporation. It is hard for us to see how it could be improved upon, and we would have expected it to go on and on, winning new converts in each generation, as indeed it has right down to the present day.

But not everyone was enraptured with conservative Calvinism. Henry Ward Beecher wasn't, although we would imagine that he would have been because his father, the Reverend Lyman Beecher, was—at the time of Henry's birth in 1813—the leading exponent of conservative Calvinistic Christianity in America, the spiritual successor to Jonathan Edwards as it were.

Robert Ingersoll describes Henry's careful Calvinistic upbringing:

"Henry Ward Beecher was born in a Puritan penitentiary," he writes, "of which his father was one of the wardens—a prison with very narrow and closely-grated windows. Under its walls were the rayless, hopeless, and measureless dungeons of the damned, and on its roof fell the shadow of God's eternal frown. In this prison the creed and the catechism were primers for children, and from a pure sense of duty their loving hearts were stained and scarred with the religion of John Calvin."

THE NEED FOR A NEW OPTION IN RELIGION

We cannot restrain our admiration for this kind of careful, doctrinally sound religious training, and deplore the negligent catechetical instruction so characteristic of our day. But we must not let our natural prejudice in favor of conservative Calvinism obscure for us the fact that by Henry Ward Beecher's time America needed another option in religion.

A wise corporation must be ever alert to sense a shift in public taste. Henry Ford was amazingly successful in the early days of automobile manufacturing, making only one model in one color. But there came a time when the Ford Motor Company was forced to offer options if it was to survive. Just so, the Christian Corporation had been doing fine with its Calvin model offered, like the Model T, in black only, up until the nineteenth century. By then, though, it was time for a change. Henry Ward Beecher's contribution to the American Christian Corporation was that he was the first of its executives to sense this need for a new model, and went ahead and produced it.

Great leaders seldom bloom overnight, though. Henry Ward Beecher did not. His first pastorate was Lawrenceburgh, Indiana, a river town which was devoted to the manufacturing of booze in those days, and for that matter still is. Upon landing this job he married his youthful sweetheart Eunice Bullard, to whom he had been engaged for seven years, just like Jacob to Rachel. Sunday after Sunday he preached away in accepted Calvinistic style, forging sermons which would convince his parishioners of their sinful condition. But he said that in three years of such preaching he "did not make a single sinner wink."

The thought occurred to him that perhaps the days of learned theological polemics in the pulpit were drawing to a close, and indeed they were because Henry Ward Beecher was going to kill them off, only neither Beecher nor the world knew this yet.

In the lives of most great men some incident, some occasion acts as a catalyst to transform them into what they are to become.

For Beecher, this was the chance attendance at a revival meeting conducted by a highly successful itinerant Methodist evangelist named John Newland Maffit. Maffit was described by one of his hearers as "a sort of pulpit actor, as well as orator." Beecher was enchanted. Here was the pulpit model he needed. He addressed himself assiduously to the aping of Maffit's platform style. From this point he progressed, almost without pause, toward becoming what he was later to be called—the archbishop of American liberal Protestantism.

Beecher reasoned—and with absolutely accurate insight we think —that his generation wasn't as hung up on religion as were the good Calvinists of his father's generation. His generation was interested, he perceived, in politics, art, business, and how to have fun. No longer, or not much longer anyway, would beautifully constructed theological architecture demonstrating the validity of the doctrine of original sin entrance the average, theologically illiterate congregation.[1] Beecher determined that he would just preach "Christ as being God because he knew how to love a sinner."

THE DANGERS OF CHRISTIANITY WITHOUT FEAR

We know that whenever the word "love" is used as descriptive of the Almighty, then here we have liberal religion. Conservative theologians bear down on God's power and justice and majesty and anger, but never love. Conservative theologians, especially Calvinists, consider a God of love as soft and squishy and effeminate. Who is afraid of a God of love? they ask. Who will go to church, and contribute to its support, and behave themselves if no one is terrorized by the threat of being tortured in an eternal hell? they demand to know.

On the face of it we would think that the conservatives had an airtight case. Removing fear of hell from religion is comparable,

[1] Henry himself was not entranced by the doctrine of original sin. He once said that for the life of him he couldn't see why the fact that Adam and Eve were once a little too frisky in the Garden of Eden insured that he was damned to hell unless God chose to relent. But then, Henry always was a little weak on doctrine.

it seems to us, to a mouthwash company deleting the graphic portrayal of the horrible social consequences of halitosis from its advertising. If no one is scared of the consequences of bad breath, who is going to buy mouthwash?

But Henry Ward Beecher had an answer. Preach the love of God in such a compelling style that people will come to church and be good Christians because they want to, instead of because you browbeat them into it, he said. And although it sounds unpromising it worked.

It was at the Second Presbyterian Church of Indianapolis, Beecher's second pastorate, that he perfected the liberal approach and style of running a Christian Corporation. The trick, when he finally discovered it, was not only to preach love, but to entertain the customers while doing it. Culture is entertaining, Beecher discovered. So are genteel reform movements. So he began lecturing on every cultural topic people wanted to hear about, and leading a number of reform movements such as projects to eliminate drunkenness, gambling, the theater, sabbath-breaking, and various other evils of a non-controversial nature.

We are saddened to learn that Beecher, though a recognized genius at the new style of doing the Lord's work, did not prosper materially as he should have according to the Protestant ethic. His congregation adored him, but it was consistently behind by a thousand dollars or so in his salary. Christian congregations, conservative or liberal, then or now, prefer to reward their pastors with adulation rather than cash.

HOW TO ORGANIZE A NEW CHURCH FOR FUN AND PROFIT

So Beecher moved east. To understand how he made the jump from frontier Indiana to the center of the civilized world, which was New York City, we must explain to you how a new church got started in those days. The truth is that in the early part of the nineteenth century churches were often organized by Christian businessmen, not only for obvious godly reasons, but also for sound business reasons.

Then, as now, church property was tax-free. A businessman, or a group of businessmen, could buy or erect a church building, hire a preacher of sufficient charm and skill to build up a big congregation, which could then pay a generous rental, and make an enormous profit. It was also possible to slip the tax collector a little something, and he wouldn't make any trouble when you rented the church for such things as public lectures, political meetings, and other profitable commercial enterprises.[2]

It happened that at about the time Beecher was growing restless in Indiana, some pious, alert businessmen organized a new church in Brooklyn, called it Plymouth Congregational Church, and instituted a search for a popular and magnetic preacher. They settled on Henry Ward Beecher.

Beecher preached his first sermon at Plymouth Church in November of 1847, without the world taking much note of it, we have to report. The papers, which were filled with sermons in those days, didn't even mention it.[3] But before long people from Brooklyn and from all the suburbs were flocking to Plymouth Church to hear the new liberal Christianity.

It was at Plymouth Church that Henry Ward Beecher at last became a national figure of the stature of Norman Vincent Peale or Billy Graham. Like Doctor Graham, Beecher was frequently mentioned as a presidential candidate, although unlike Doctor Graham—who appears to have no political aspirations—Beecher held himself in readiness to heed the call of his country if it ever came, which unfortunately it didn't. Again like Doctor Graham, Beecher had the ear of the president, in this case Abraham Lincoln. But again unlike Doctor Graham, who is a good buddy of President Nixon, as he was of President Johnson and President Eisenhower, Lincoln was not taken with Beecher. Lincoln privately called him a mountebank and a pretentious windbag, and had as little to do with him as possible. We admit that Beecher affected a florid

[2] One authority reports that, in those days, a church in a good location was far more profitable than grade-A rail or utility stocks.

[3] The papers did report that, on the evening before Beecher was installed, Mrs. Beecher was mugged in the streets and robbed, which shows that Brooklyn hasn't changed as much as we would have expected it to in the intervening years.

style, but we think this very unfair of Mr. Lincoln. Perhaps his
distaste for Beecher was because Mr. Lincoln was partial, he said,
to preachers who, when in the pulpit, appeared to be fighting a
swarm of bees.

One vital instinct necessary to a popular preacher is the instinct
that detects what is popular at the moment, or shortly will be
popular. No one has ever surpassed Henry Ward Beecher in the
keenness of this detecting apparatus. He refrained from hasty
commitment on the slavery issue, but when his sister published
Uncle Tom's Cabin, and the owners of his church were leaning
toward abolition, he detected that the time had come for him to
take a courageous stand on the question. He went to England
to convince the English that slavery was wrong.[4] He auctioned
off slave girls from the proscenium of Plymouth Church,[5] which
garnered reams of excellent publicity for the cause of abolition,
and also for Beecher, of course. He drew overflow crowds to
Plymouth Church and to his lectures, and wrote articles for national
magazines on slavery as well as other popular subjects. He wrote
best-selling books.[6]

It warms our hearts to read that, at long last, Beecher began
to reap the financial rewards which our theology assures us will
accrue to the diligent and deserving righteous. Plymouth Church
was paying him a salary of twenty thousand dollars a year. Only
a handful of preachers are paid that kind of money even in these
inflationary days, and in the middle of the nineteenth century no
other preacher was even near that figure. He was able to supple-
ment his basic income with fabulous fees for lectures, and exceedingly
generous royalty checks from his writings.

Only one incident beclouded Beecher's reputation during these
great days for liberal Christianity. One of his church members,
Theodore Tilton by name, charged that Beecher had seduced Mrs.

---

[4] They were already convinced.
[5] They were very pretty, light-skinned slave girls.
[6] Beecher himself was not fond of reading, except maybe the dictionary
which, while weak on plot, contained many fine polysyllabic words which
sounded dandy in sermons. It is doubtful, some biographers say, if he ever
read a book through in his entire life. But he thought reading books was very
cultural and uplifting for other people, so he wrote a lot of books.

Tilton, and sued him for alienation of affection. Nothing ever came of it though, except that the trial received national and international publicity, as everyone knows how people like to savor even a morsel of scandal about famous figures. The charge was never proved, Beecher drew larger crowds than ever to Plymouth Church, and the distasteful incident lingered on only in the form of a little ditty the children sometimes sang in the streets of Brooklyn which said:

> Beecher, Beecher is my name—
> Beecher till I die!
> I never kissed Mis' Tilton—
> I never told a lie!

BEECHER ABOLISHES HELL

Let us, then, recapitulate. Henry Ward Beecher contributed to the building of the new American Christian Corporation the concept of liberal Christianity as a socially acceptable option to conservative Christianity. He established love as one of God's legitimate attributes simply by saying he favored it. He abolished hell for Christians of a liberal persuasion simply by saying he was against it. He employed publicity and public relations gimmickry as devices for building the kingdom of God on earth and thus made such flamboyant techniques respectable. He showed by example that a preacher doesn't have to be poor to be pious, and powerful in the works of righteousness—although it is easier to convince preachers that this is true than it is to convince congregations, and most congregations still don't believe it is possible.

We must, of course, be realistic in our assessment of Henry Ward Beecher and avoid overpraising him. Although he made it possible for us today to be liberal Christians and be intellectually fashionable as well as socially approved while being such, we now know that Beecher's Christian liberalism was an early, crude form of Christian liberalism.

For example, in Beecher's time you could be a theological liberal simply by not believing in hell. Today, just not believing in hell

is inadequate. Today to be a theological liberal in good standing
it is necessary not to believe in God.

Take another example. It was bold liberal Christianity for Beecher
to sell slave girls from the pulpit. But today we would be aware
that this is only tokenism. Modern liberal Christians know that
trying to relate personally to blacks, or indulge ourselves in works
of humaneness and mercy and good will, is only a mask for our
vicious racism. Today's liberals know that you have to solve the
problem of slavery, or segregation as we call it, holding seminars
and with articles in *The New Republic,* and through infinitely
large government bureaus manned by liberals. Christian liberalism,
we can see, has come a long way since Henry Ward Beecher.

LIBERAL AND CONSERVATIVE CHRISTIANITY CONTRASTED

The distinguishing characteristic of liberal Christianity is that it
tells you exactly what is good for you, and what isn't. This is also
the distinguishing characteristic of conservative Christianity. However, what conservative Christianity thinks is good for you is what
liberal Christianity thinks is bad for you.

Conservative Christians, for example, claim creeds and doctrines
are good for you, but that to fiddle around with changing the
social structure and improve the lot of the starving masses is bad
for you as well as bad for Christianity. We should note, however,
that conservative Christians are frequently kind and generous to
indigent individuals of whom they approve,[7] and will send them
baskets of groceries at Christmastime or a turkey for Thanksgiving,
but are unalterably opposed to socialistic schemes such as the
guaranteed annual wage or socialized medicine. Liberal Christians,
on the other hand, think creeds and doctrines are bad for you,
but for Christianity to remake the social order so that we will
have a more just society is good for you. Liberal Christians are

---

[7] "The deserving poor" is a favorite conservative Christian phrase. By this,
conservative Christians mean the poor who are respectful to the rich, and
properly grateful for anything their masters dole out to them. Today there
are so few of the poor who, by this standard, qualify as "deserving" that
they are hardly a problem.

always terribly concerned for the masses, but personal experience with liberal Christians will lead you to the conclusion that many of them don't care much for individual people.

We are all most grateful, naturally, that liberal Christianity has shown us that we must be flexible Christians. They have told us for ages that we white Christians are sinners because we have practiced segregation of the races. However, we are told that black people are definitely not sinners when they advocate black separatism, which we would have thought was segregation of the races, unless liberal Christians had explained to us that it isn't the same thing at all. The same is true of the practice of some rich white people of resorting to force and violence to make people do what they want, which liberal Christians agree is a great evil. We jumped to the conclusion that resorting to force and violence is always evil, but liberal Christians have told us that this isn't the case, that force and violence are terribly Christian when employed by poor black people or the Students for a Democratic Society. It is doubtful if we would have been able to understand all those important distinctions without the aid of liberal Christianity—and we owe it all to Henry Ward Beecher.

To sum up: what we have, then, in the new American Christian Corporation as of today, are two parallel strains of Christian theology and practice—the conservative strain flowing from Jonathan Edwards, and the liberal tradition founded by Henry Ward Beecher.

There are, of course, almost infinite variations within each tradition, and we view this as a distinct asset to the Corporation—something like being able to order your new Dodge with or without disc brakes, vinyl top, or the superhot engine, as you see fit. Today, whatever your belief—whether mild or wild, sensible or irrational, logical or just plain nutty, you can find a congenial spiritual haven among people who think as you think and do as you do, somewhere within the confines of the Christian Corporation.

XXI. *The modern ecumenical movement—or the American Christian Corporation confidently confronts the future*

We have now traced for you the story of the Christian Corporation from the time it became a true corporation under the Emperor Constantine, through its ups and downs over the centuries, down to its establishment here in America. The moment has come for us to survey its present state, and assay its prospects for the future.

For the purposes of our study we must exclude any consideration of the Roman Catholic branch of the American Church. We do this not through sectarian malice, heaven forbid, but because the Roman Church is, at the moment, completely engrossed in wrestling with the problems of papal authority, celibacy of the clergy, liturgical reform, the preservation of Thomistic theology, and other arcane concerns which are not relevant to anything we care about, and which apparently will monopolize its time and energy for generations to come, so it won't be able to do much of anything else in the foreseeable future. As of now, then, we must look upon the Protestant churches in America as the true Christian Corporation in this country. It is to the problem of shaping them into a proper corporation that we address ourselves.

DENOMINATIONAL COMPETITION PROMOTES HEALTHY GROWTH

We must begin by facing the fact that American Protestantism is drenched in denominationalism. As we have seen, these various sects calling themselves churches originated with the holiest of motivations, which was to carry the truth to the people. In the days when each denomination was convinced that it alone had apprehended divine truth, the competition was fierce, which created a climate of healthy growth for all denominations.

Let us recall how the system worked. The Presbyterian and Reformed churches would regale their customers with unimpeachable arguments as to the necessity for believing in predestination, infant damnation, and other glories of Calvinistic theology. The Methodists, and other churches of the Arminian[1] persuasion just as enthusiastically extolled the virtues of man's own initiative in finding his way to hell.

But with each passing generation there is a diminution in the desire to debate doctrine. Today even the clergy of the various sects is a little hazy as to what exactly is the distinctive truth which created its denomination in the first place. And hardly any laymen —of the main-line churches anyway—join a particular communion because, say, they feel strongly for or against supralapsarianism.

While many deplore the evaporation of distinctive denominational doctrines, and lament the demise of the acrimonious debates over theological propositions which did so much to enliven church life and promote sectarian loyalty, we may as well face the fact that this day is gone, never to return.

What we must do, obviously, is to find a substitute, some other basis for the promotion of the Christian Corporation. This has been apparent for some years now to our more knowledgeable denominational leaders. Though for the purpose of encouraging the loyalty of those adherents of denominationalism who still believe there are distinguishable doctrinal differences between sects these leaders

---

[1] A few of our readers may be unfamiliar with the term "Arminian," and indeed confuse it with "Armenian," which is an entirely different thing. Arminianism is a theology which says that God would like it better if everyone got to heaven, although He is dubious about it working out that way. Calvinism, on the other hand, says that of course God doesn't want everyone in heaven and selects only those He finds congenial, sending all the rest to hell for His greater glory. Arminianism, which gets its name from Jacob Arminius who preached it, is—you will be glad to know—opposed to supralapsarianism, and leans toward infralapsarian views. Obviously, though, Arminianism is pallid stuff when compared to Calvinism.

pretend that such differences do exist, they know that this is not the case, and have wisely discarded the whole concept. They are, instead, working frantically to create a reformed Christian Corporation in which all denominations will be welded into one massive organization. The name for this effort is "The Ecumenical Movement."

ECUMENISM—A BRILLIANT BUSINESS STRATEGY

Our sober, responsible judgment of the idea of putting all the middling and big sects together to form one whopping denomination must be that it is brilliance itself, a stroke of sheer genius! Not only does it fit in with the business temper of the times, which is all for profitable mergers, but it is a resurrection in modern form of the Holy Roman Empire.

We know from our study that the Holy Roman Empire was mostly a myth, and never really existed except in men's minds. But this is unimportant. If men believe in a myth, which they did in the myth of the Holy Roman Empire, it doesn't make any difference whether it is true or not.[2] And when you can marry a myth to a practical business proposition, which is the case with the Ecumenical Movement, you are almost bound to win.

The Ecumenical Movement is presently embodied in an organization called Consultation on Church Union, or COCU for short (which is not the most fortunate acronym we ever heard). It consists of most of the main-line sects such as Presbyterian, Congregational, Methodist, Episcopalian, and some denominations you haven't heard much about. It is still in the talk stage, which is only what we would expect, because it wasn't proposed until maybe about ten years ago. But when it finally gets going, COCU intends to have a monopoly on the faith business in the U.S.A., and we certainly can find no fault with this intent because expansion is not only very American but also the soul of progress.

So far, progress toward COCU's goal has been heartening if not

2 We had determined to resist the temptation to remind you that the Holy Roman Empire was neither holy, Roman, nor an empire, but we decided to tell you because, if we don't, you might think we didn't know it.

spectacular. Some balky denominations, such as the Lutherans and the Baptists, have not as yet joined up, it is true. However, one can envision a time in the not too distant future when COCU will be so overwhelming in size and power that no self-respecting denomination can stay out of it.

HOW TO TRANSLATE ECCLESIASTICAL PRONOUNCEMENTS INTO EASY ENGLISH

Futhermore, the consultations got off on the right foot, sounded the appropriate note. In its document *Principles of Church Union* COCU states:

"We resolve to attempt . . . (an) inclusive expression of the oneness of the Church . . . It means *an increase in corporate strength* (italics ours), not alone in numbers but also in the vitality of common witness."

We are aware that the lay mind is not conditioned to comprehend the rich, full prose style of ecclesiastical documents. What this passage means is "We haven't been doing too well lately going it on our own, so why don't we get together, cut overhead costs, and streamline our operation?" It would never do to say it outright, though, as church people are accustomed to pompous nomenclature, and prefer that even the most practical proposition come wrapped in rotund pious syllables.

The same document states: "Obedience to mission must be the primary characteristic of the Church at every level." Evidently even some of the drafting committee felt that, lovely as it is, the phrase is a little vague for the average Christian laymen, so an explanation follows which reads in part: "This refers, of course, to our plain duty to eliminate overlapping duplication so that greater energies can be released for the common task." Any ecclesiastical bureaucrat would translate this to mean, "We've got too much dead wood in the personnel of our boards and agencies, and some people are going to be looking for jobs."[3]

[3] Ecclesiastical bureaucrats are almost exclusively ordained clergy. When they have to look for a job it usually means they must return to the parish

Some other passages from this significant and commendable document, along with translations, are:

"Visible unity should take away from us nothing except our separateness, and add to our common treasury." Translation: "It will save us a lot of dough to do it this way."

"The costs of a wider unity will doubtless require sacrifices on the part of all, including the acceptance of new limitations for the common good. Structures of authority are necessary . . ." Translation: "There's going to be a shakeup, but if you think you are going to get rid of a visible, highly organized power structure, you're crazy."

"The majority should not coerce the minority, nor should the minority willfully obstruct conscientious action by the majority." Translation: "We are going to listen patiently to the crackpots before doing as we damn please."

The statement says that in the matter of creeds the new Christian Corporation will use the Apostles' Creed because it is "shaped by biblical language and resonant with biblical testimonies." It says that COCU will also use the Nicene creed because "through many critical periods it has successfully warned the Church against many deceptive distortions in its faith."[4] The statement goes on to say that "the responsibility of the united Church as guardian of the apostolic testimony[5] includes its obligation, from time to time, to confess and communicate its faith in new language and new formulations . . ."

Here the untutored layman is likely to bog down completely. What is being said, though, is relatively simple. The correct reading is, "Some people like the sound of the Apostles' Creed, and others have a sense of being orthodox when they repeat the intricate verbosities of the Nicene Creed, so we will dish up both creeds

---

ministry—a prospect few of them can face with equanimity. This is why the incidence of ulcers, nervous collapse, and other diseases of psychic origin is so high among this class of church leader.

[4] Church councils do not shy away from redundancy when they can come up with a sonorous and alliterative phrase such as "deceptive distortions."

[5] The apostolic testimony is the same thing as the apostolic tradition which, as we have seen, the popes have been guarding since the early centuries of the Christian Corporation.

in our services from time to time. On the other hand, since no sane modern man can affirm either of these creeds literally without compromising his conscience, we will write some new creeds which won't offend him. This way, maybe we can keep everybody happy."

So far, we can but shout "hurrah!" for the statements in this document of principles for the new American Christian Corporation as envisioned by the Consultation on Church Union. They are sound. They are practical. They are useful. Though making admirable use of the style and nomenclature peculiar to ecclesiastical documents, they are every bit the equal of business communications in obscure and unintelligible rhetoric. They are very, very good.

THE SACRED AND HISTORIC OFFICE OF BISHOP RETAINED

To continue our praise of the sagacious decisions already made by COCU, it flatly states, "The united Church accepts the office of bishop." It goes ahead to spell out his responsibilities. These shall include "administrative responsibility," at which he shall be assisted by a corps of assistants and subadministrators and specialists of one kind and another. The exact number of assistants to be provided each bishop in the COCU-plan Church is not specified, but we can be assured that it will be very large to begin with, and that it will grow with the years. Ecclesiastical organizations fall victims to Parkinson's Law quicker than any other type of business.

Our readers are already rejoicing, we imagine, that COCU has affirmed its faith in an hierarchical church structure, a type of organization sanctified by ecclesiastical tradition, and proven so effective in practice. A Christian Corporation without a clearly defined power structure would be unable to make planning and policy decisions at the top level to be handed down and enforced by the middle and lower levels of its officialdom. It could not levy financial assessments on the laity and make them stick. It could not reward its faithful and obedient employees with better jobs and better titles, and punish its fractious and rebellious minions and mavericks in all the painful ways available to a hierarchical organization. We would have no confidence in the future of COCU had it not opted for the bishop system of church structure.

The planners of the Consultation on Church Union said, not long ago, that it anticipated that ten more years of talking about church union would be required before any really concrete steps can be taken. At first blush this seems to us an excessive amount of talking. But there are two sound reasons behind the decision.

One reason is that it allays the fears of the good Christian laymen who, almost to a person, think church union is a glorious idea—but not in their denomination or in their congregation—and especially not now. If COCU announced that it was really getting down to business in twelve months from now, pandemonium would reign and everyone would come up with obstacles to union which couldn't be overcome except through years of study and reports and conferences. Nobody worries, though, about what is going to happen in ten years, as demonstrated by our public complacency about the problems of pollution and population explosion, which we know are going to do us in—but not just yet.

The other reason is that the present denominational bureaucrats, of which there are thousands, would never consent to any changes to begin in less than ten years. As in all hierarchies—civil, business or religious—the bureaucracy actually runs things, and in the end always gets its way. They have their niches in the present structure comfortably carved out and battened down. Those who retire within this ten-year period do not wish to be disturbed. Those who don't must have that much time to jockey for position in the new COCU bureaucracy.

There are those, of course, who clamor for speedier action. They claim that ten years is too long to wait, that the world moves rapidly these days, and that in another ten years there may be so little left of the churches that uniting them would be similar to tying several corpses together.

THE PONDEROUS PACE OF CHRISTIAN SOLDIERS

We must not listen to their strident voices. Those who have
read this book realize that the Christian Corporation, in any age,
moves with deliberate speed. Admittedly this ponderous pace does
have disadvantages. The average church convention or conference,
for example, is normally found taking forthright action on questions
which were burning issues five to fifty years ago, and hence no
longer require any action, as nothing the Church can do now
makes any difference anyway. On the other hand, this strategy
prevents the Church from committing itself prematurely to precip-
itate and untested courses of action. Also, answering questions
the world is no longer asking offends no one, and thus is excellent
public relations for the Christian Corporation.

The new Christian Corporation in process of formation, or COCU,
also needs at least ten years to debate the theology of ordination.
We can expect this, because the Christian Corporation has been
debating it almost since the time of Constantine, and there is no
apparent reason why it should stop now. Not everyone is familiar
with the theology of ordination, so perhaps we should explain that
it has to do with apostolic succession, and sacerdotal duties and
privileges, and other esoteric and antic[6] questions which strike the
ordinary unlearned layman as not too germane to the business at
hand. You will just have to take our word for it, we suppose,
that the theology of ordination is central and vital and well worthy
of a decade of debate by COCU, although we can't tell you
exactly why, because only a thoroughly tutored specialist in the
nature of ordination is able to explain why it is so important.

Ten years is also all too short a time for the builders of COCU
to discuss the structure of the new Christian Corporation. As we
have already told you, it has decided to have bishops and a
hierarchical structure. The non-reflective man might jump to the
conclusion that the structure, then, is already set and ready to go.

Not so. There is an immense amount of talking to be done

---

[6] "Antic" can mean odd, grotesque, fantastic or ludicrous. Take your choice.

about number of executives, job titles, who reports to whom, how much of a voice and influence to permit laymen and how this is to be handled,[7] executives' salary structure and vacation policy— an almost endless list of important issues to be decided.

Anyway, "structure" is the newest word in the lexicon of piety. It is not yet, perhaps, equal with "mission," "relevance," and "involvement," but it is coming up fast, and those who are shaping COCU utter it in hushed and solemn tones appropriate to a high mass or grade-A funeral parlor.

You can now see why we say the New American Christian Corporation confronts the future with confidence. The horizon looked dark indeed when the old, fierce denominational competition faded away as a motive for being loyal to a church. But the Ecumenical Movement has dispelled the clouds of gloom, and is promising to cast the bright warm sunshine of prosperity once more on the Corporation.

Up to now the Corporation's plans for the future have our heartiest approval. No fair-minded man can rightly criticize them. However, we see one flaw, one big, blooming, horrendous mistake in COCU's concept which its leaders have overlooked, and which —if uncorrected—could well doom the entire project. In the next chapter, then, we shall point out this mistake and provide an alternative plan which cannot possibly fail. We know that the Consultation on Church Union, and the entire American Christian Corporation will be deeply grateful to us.

---

[7] This is not exactly the way to summarize the question of how much influence to grant laymen in the new Corporation. In any hierarchical system this decision has already been made—the influence of the layman is very small. The problem is to devise the best way to make the influence of the layman appear to be very large, while in no way affecting the policy or operation of the Corporation.

XXII. *The solid gold surplice*

We are now ready to offer our own plan to the Consultation on Church Union as to how it can patch together dozens of denominations into one huge, rich, powerful and awesome American Christian Corporation. We do this because, as noted in the last chapter, the leaders of COCU are about to make a mistake of monumental dimensions, and it is our desire to save them from this.

The mistake COCU is making lies in the model they are imitating. We fear that its leaders have cast their eyes over the history of the Church, and have decided on the Holy Roman Empire as the pattern for the New American Christian Corporation.

Since we yield to none in our admiration for the Holy Roman Empire, we can understand the mistake. The HRE was a vast and powerful Christian Corporation. It is only natural, then, that COCU would seek weld the splinters and fragments which we call denominations into one mighty enterprise. Dazzled by the magnificence of the HRE, they intend to recreate it on American soil.

But there is a better way. There is a superior model. When it comes to growth potential, power, efficiency of operation, pyramiding hierarchical executive structure, the ability to gobble up markets, glamor, wealth, and favorable public image, no organization in human history can compete with the large American business corporation. Our suggestion, then, is for COCU to pick the most successful of American business corporations and build the New American Christian Corporation by emulating it. Let us show you how this would work.

THE MODEL FOR THE NEW AMERICAN CHRISTIAN CORPORATION

Picking our model corporation is easy. Among all the admirable business corporations which have blessed American life, one stands out. It is, of course, General Motors. GM is the synonym for corporate success—and a corporate success is what the New American Christian Corporation[1] wants to be above all other things.

Let us, then, examine the philosophy and operation of General Motors Corporation for clues as to how we shall build a truly effective NACC.

Let us begin by asking, "What is fundamental to GM's spectacular success?" The Holy Roman Empire succeeded because it presented to the public a monolith, a monopoly with no competition permitted. It was effective in its time, we admit, but styles have changed. Americans cherish as sacred the concept of business competition. Aware of this, General Motors promotes internal competition within the corporation itself, but sees to it that all the power and all the money end up at one place. This is precisely what the New American Christian Corporation must do.

HOW GENERAL MOTORS SELLS INTANGIBLES

We find that we have a felicitous analogy when we compare the product of GM and NACC. Both deal in intangibles. Some will protest that GM sells vehicles for transportation, a tangible

[1] Following the current custom of referring to organizations by their acronymous designation, we will henceforth say NACC when we mean the New American Christian Corporation. NACC has a nice sound to it, we think. Also, it is a phonetic rendering of "knack," and knack" is something we hope the New American Christian Corporation will have. Anyway, it is a better acronym than COCU. COCU wants to call the new church "the Church of Christ Uniting," but the acronym for this is also COCU.

product. GM quit doing that a long time ago. When it discovered that one automobile is very much like another automobile, and that any automobile will provide adequate transportation, GM went into the business of selling dreams, wish fulfillment, sexual fantasies, social prestige, image-building, and all sorts of intangible goods, which it packaged and called an automobile.

Now let us look at the product of the Christian Corporation. As we have seen, it originally went into business to purvey salvation. Salvation was a tangible product. When the Church was satisfied that you qualified for it, the corporation guaranteed your salvation, sometimes even giving you a certificate, as in the case of an indulgence. But readers of this book will recall that Martin Luther ruined all that. He said salvation goes along with being a Christian, but that God gives it directly to you, not the corporation. Luther was as disruptive of the Christian Corporation as Ralph Nader has been of General Motors Corporation.

The average American today, then, expects salvation when he joins a church, but he expects a lot more. He is in the market for social identity, congenial social contacts, and profitable business contacts. He wants religious pageantry appropriate to his level of taste, culture, and social status to mark the arrival of his offsprings, the nuptials for his daughters, and his own departure from this mortal scene. He wants people to be able to tell, by the brand name of the church he attends, the kind of fellow he is. We now perceive that the Church, like GM, deals in intangibles, and the packaging and marketing of religion differs hardly at all from the marketing of automobiles.[2]

---

[2] It may be that some people will credit us with thinking up the comparison of religion with business. We wish we had, but we must disclaim originating this brilliant concept. The late Bruce Barton, an advertising genius, is thought to have been the first to grasp that Jesus was the prototype of the hustling, up-and-coming, out-to-win business executive who was a superb salesman of his ideas. Many eminent divines—far too many to mention by name, in fact— have told us for the past quarter century that Christianity is simply a matter of packaging and selling a very special product.

GENERAL MOTORS REJECTS THE HOLY ROMAN EMPIRE

General Motors could have, had it wished to do so, modeled itself after the Holy Roman Empire. No doubt at some moment in GM's history an aggressive executive suggested, "Why don't we model ourselves after the Holy Roman Empire? Then we could produce just one model, thereby cutting costs, and raising prices, thereby increasing profits. Let's eliminate all this foolishness of giving people choices." But he was overruled. Wiser executives knew that, while everyone is in the market for the same goods, you can't sell everyone the same package.

GM knows, furthermore, that while in this democratic society of ours every man is the equal of every other man, there is in practice a marked difference between people in such things as wealth, taste, influence, cultural level, etc. Or to put it another way, we do have unadmitted but nonetheless clearly defined and universally recognized layers or laminations which carry rather precise assignments of status in our society. The recognition of this truth accounts for GM's success as a merchandiser.

Let us look at how GM goes about selling its product. It knows that there is no appreciable difference, in terms of transportation, between a Chevrolet and a Cadillac. But as a badge of your status in our society the difference is almost immeasurable. So GM takes a basic automobile, which it calls a Chevrolet. Then it beefs up the basic carcass of the car, lays on a few millimeters extra of padding in the upholstery and covers it with a costly tapestry cloth instead of Fabrikoid or whatever, knocks off some of the Chevrolet pizzaz such as chrome curlicues and puffy wheel covers —items which the lower classes find so appealing but the upper classes consider vulgar—and calls the creation a Cadillac. Then, between Chevrolet and Cadillac, it alters the process enough to manufacture other makes—more luxurious than a Chevrolet, but less desirable than a Cadillac—all matched to a certain level of status and affluence in our society. This, we submit, is genius in the merchandising of intangibles.

THE PEACE OF MIND WHICH ACCOMPANIES
OWNERSHIP OF A MONOPOLY

Awestruck as we are by the cleverness of this sales strategy, GM's real genius is best seen, we think, in its actual selling technique. What it does is to organize each make of car as a separate company, then tells each one to get out and hustle and outsell the other makes in the GM family. A corporation can only do this, naturally, if it doesn't care which division wins because it enjoys the serenity and peace of mind which comes from knowing that all the profits will end up at the same place anyway. We are pleased to recall that St. Paul told the Corinthians that while the body has many members it is, finally, one body. This makes the GM plan consistent with the Scriptures, and it is always nice if you can be consistent with the Scriptures.

Another facet of GM's brilliance is its understanding that not everyone would want to begin their car ownership with a Cadillac, even if they could afford it. Many people would be uncomfortable in a car unsuited to their station in life. But this is a mobile society, and a certain number of Chevrolet owners eventually will aspire to be Cadillac owners. You can't, however, jump right out of a Chevrolet into a Cadillac. The rise is too sharp. The change is so radical, psychologically, as to be traumatic. The way to do it, GM thinks, is to graduate from a Chevrolet to a Pontiac to a Buick or Oldsmobile, and ultimately arrive at a Cadillac—and of course GM is right.

What we have, then, in General Motors, is a corporation structured to capture a near-monopolistic share of the business at every level of a man's psychological needs. We want to structure the New American Christian Corporation, or NACC, so that it can serve every level of man's spiritual needs.[3] We want NACC to be a near-monopoly, yet preserving all the zing infused into American church life by denominational competition.

[3] We admit that "can serve" is a euphemism for "capture the business." However, it is better to use "can serve" than "capture the business" when speaking of the spiritual because it is common, familiar, churchy nomenclature, and people are conditioned to respond favorably to familiar churchy talk.

THE ERROR IN CHURCH UNION

We are now in a position to see what a terrible mistake the Consultation on Church Union is making by attempting to melt down all the sects adhering to it into one denomination. This is analogous to General Motors trying to make all car owners accept a Chevrolet. It simply goes against human nature. Not everyone wants a Chevrolet, and there are those who do not want a Chevrolet religion. Neither does everyone want a Cadillac, or a Cadillac religion. For example, we all know people who don't want to be Episcopalians, though Episcopalianism is undeniably the Cadillac of American religion, even if they could be one.

THE NEW AMERICAN CHRISTIAN CORPORATION ORGANIZATIONAL CHART

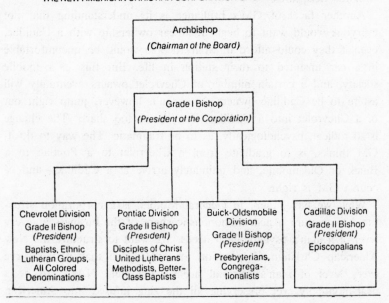

Now that we have convinced you that wisdom's only course is to make NACC a replica of GM, let us turn to a study of how this is to be accomplished.

General Motors Corporation has a chairman of the board. For purposes of clarity, we may think of the chairman of the board as the business equivalent of the pope. Then GM has a president, who is the chief executive officer for the corporation, comparable, we suppose, to the cardinal-archbishop who presides over the *curia*. Then, under the president, each division of GM has its own president. Refer now, please, to the accompanying chart, and observe how the GM plan can be applied to the construction of the New American Christian Corporation.

You will notice that as chairman of the board we have placed an, or more accurately *the* archbishop, as in our proposed plan there would be only one archbishop. He is the pope of NACC. We are afraid, though, that good, solid American Protestants— especially those in the Chevrolet and Pontiac divisions—would find the title "pope" disturbing. However, "archbishop" is not nearly so offensive, and since we have to call our top churchman something to distinguish him from bishops of a lower grade, archbishop is the best option we have.

THE JOYS OF BEING ARCHBISHOP OF NACC

To be archbishop of the New American Christian Corporation would be an exalted position indeed! We need only let our imaginations play with the possibilities of the office to envision our top leader pronouncing from his seat of authority what the Church thinks about everything from Eldridge Cleaver to the Christian length for miniskirts. He would be a confidant of presidents on a par with Billy Graham. Perhaps most importantly, the very existence of his office would offer ample motivation to all upward-striving clergymen to strive harder, because they would be able to picture themselves in the position. They would look on the archbishopric as the ultimate goal and reward for those found worthy of large leadership and the exercise of incalculable power. The archbishop of NACC would be somebody—an American pope at last, except for his title.

Since ecclesiastical authority depends so heavily on the backing of tradition, it will be necessary to supply the office of archbishop of NACC with instant tradition. Tradition has to do with rites and residences and ring-kissing, things like that. We expect that NACC will want to set up a department of protocol and procedure which can amuse itself with establishing the details of instant tradition.[4]

We do, however, have one contribution we wish to make to the tradition with which we hope NACC will soon be entrusted. It is in the matter of the archbishop's costume or garb. Nothing does more to lend weight and authority to a churchly office than the appropriate clothing of its occupant.

Our archbishop, like the pope, must appear in garments which no one else is permitted to imitate. However, since we are a democratic society with a built-in prejudice against the gaudy and the bizarre, we must walk a narrow line in designing high-priestly haberdashery which will at the same time signify magnificence and humility.

For everyday wear we suggest that, as bishops traditionally affect a red or purple *rabat* (clerical shirt), our archbishop may follow this well-established custom. But let his clerical shirt be of a special hue, perhaps cerise or mauve, which only he may display.

The same principle of humble elegance should be our guide when selecting the archbishop's ceremonial habiliments. When performing priestly functions requiring sacerdotal garb, a simple cassock and surplice—the garments of the humblest celebrant—should be worn. But the archbishop's surplice should be made of the finest cloth of gold. By wearing the surplice, a plain, nightgownlike garment, he symbolizes the humility befitting a priest. By wearing a garment of costly gold cloth he reminds the world of the wealth, power and pre-eminence of the New American Christian Corporation. A solid gold surplice seems to us a most fitting symbol of the New American Christian Corporation.

---

[4] It may seem to some of our readers that the establishment of instant tradition is a formidable task. This, happily, is not the case. Most people haven't the vaguest idea as to when the traditions of their school or lodge or church were originated. The important point is that they believe them to be traditions. Our research indicates that when an organization does something a certain way for approximately one year, people begin to say, "we've always done it this way."

THE VALUE OF LOW-GRADE BISHOPS

We shall leave it to NACC to brevet the other bishops of various grades in the hierarchy. Suffice to say that the president-bishop is a No. 1 grade bishop, and the presidents of the various divisions are No. 2 grade bishops. Each No. 2 grade bishop will have under him, of course, a passel of Nos. 3, 4, 5 and 6 grade bishops. There is, in fact, no theoretic limit as to how low in grade an executive may be and still be designated bishop. This plan is similar to the business practice—common at GM and all other large American corporations—of granting nearly all male employees above the rank of office boy the title of vice-president. Everyone in the company knows that there is a great deal of difference between one vice-president and another. But people on the outside are vague about it, and think highly of any vice-president. This helps morale, and also saves the company money because a title is often more prized than a raise in salary. NACC will need to keep this in mind. It is bound to have financing problems. If, then, it can obtain adequate manpower to perform its menial chores by offering clergymen the coveted title of bishop, even a grade 6 bishop or even lower, in lieu of a decent salary, it will help no end.[5]

Now let us refer once more to our organizational chart. We have, as you can see, reduced our divisions from the GM plan of five to a NACC plan of four. The reason for our reduction is that in GM the Buick and the Oldsmobile divisions cover approximately the same segment of the market. There was a time, as we all know, when Buick outranked Oldsmobile. But the desirability of a Buick Electra over an Oldsmobile 98 today is so infinitesimal as to be lost on the average customer. Our market studies have shown that, by the same token, Presbyterianism and Congregationalism have almost equal appeal to the same customer-group level. There is, then, no apparent reason for separating them into two divisions.

[5] Recall that at one time the Church ordained its janitors instead of paying them.

SORTING OUT THE DENOMINATIONS

Now let us survey the denominational groupings in the divisions. At the lower end we have Baptists, ethnic Lutheran sects,[6] and all colored denominations.[7] We hope these denominations will take no offense at being placed at the bottom of the scale. We remind them that a Chevrolet is a fine car. It is dependable and will do the job. Though it carries no cachet of class, and no one brags that he drives a Chevrolet, Chevrolets are absolutely essential. There are more of them than any other make. And just as the Chevrolet division is the most profitable of all GM divisions, so the New American Christian Corporation can anticipate the bulk of its income from its Chevrolet division.

In the Pontiac division we find the Disciples of Christ, which laps back into the Chevrolet division. We also find here the Methodists—or United Methodists as they are now known, since they have absorbed several smaller sects in recent years. This denomination belongs partly in the Buick-Oldsmobile division because it is the denomination with the most upward mobility. It is moving up fast. Indeed, we can foresee the time when it may have to be moved to the Buick-Oldsmobile division, especially in the South. But not yet.

The Buick-Oldsmobiles of American denominations are the Presbyterians and the Congregationalists. They aren't quite Cadillacs,

---

[6] The author is aware that the Lutherans and the Baptists are not yet a part of the Consultation on Church Union. We include non-COCU denominations in our chart because of our firm faith that, once COCU becomes NACC, it will prove irresistible to most sects, and there will be a grand rush to get in.

[7] We mean no racial slur here. But colored people, though we appreciate their grand sense of rhythm and athletic prowess, do not as yet confer any status to an organization by belonging to it. Those pictures we see in the newspapers and on TV of white congregations linking arms to keep colored worshipers out of their church are often misinterpreted as examples of Christian racism. They aren't that at all. What these good white Christians are trying to do is to preserve the character and status level of their beloved church. We regret that the public does not always understand this.

and they aren't ever going to be. But from a distance it is hard to tell the difference. It is perfectly proper to boast of being one.

The Episcopalians are like Cadillacs—they are in a class by themselves. There is nothing else which bespeaks taste, breeding, wealth, refinement, membership in the establishment, high position, social impeccability, immaculate genealogy, and other things every American wishes were his, like owning a Cadillac or being an Episcopalian. NACC must not forget that most people hope to move up as their social standings and bank accounts improve with the years. Just as GM nags at us to "move up" to this or that make of car, so NACC must make the transition from, for example, the Southern Baptists to the Congregationalists easy and attractive.

We think we have outlined here a plan for the New American Christian Corporation so rich in promise and possibilities as to dispel your gloom concerning the future of the Church.

Those Cassandras prophesying an early demise of the Church tell us that, as now constituted, the Church is decimated by public indifference, and that it is underfinanced because of escalation in costs of doing business and at the same time suffering from plummeting revenues. They point out what they see as the appalling mediocrity of church leadership. They cite the alarming slippage in Sunday school attendance.[8] They refer to a clutch, or at least a pride of other sorrows.

While we would not deny that there is some truth in these contentions, readers of this book—now possessing a perspective on the history of the Church—will recognize these present symptoms as by no means terminal. It is just another of those temporary low periods which, from time to time throughout its history, have beset the Christian institution. Like influenza or the three-day measles, it will pass. After all, even at General Motors some years are less profitable than others.

---

[8] We do share these critics' concern over the decline of the Sunday school, because—by tradition—the Sunday school has been the propaganda arm of the Church. It does impart, it is true, a smattering of religious instruction, but this is peripheral to its main purpose which, other than providing a cheap and convenient baby-sitting service, is to inculcate denominational loyalty.

THE IMPORTANCE OF POSITIVE THINKING

What we must do, at this juncture in Christian history, is to discard all negative thoughts about the state of the Church. Agreed as we are that we must conceive of the Church as a corporation, let us cheer ourselves up with a brief review of its present corporate assets.

PLANT

Nothing will do so much for our morale as recalling the multibillion-dollar plant now in the possession of the present American Christian Corporation.

Think of the church buildings alone. They number well over one hundred thousand. True, many of them are small, unimpressive frame structures in the rural and small town areas. But thousands of them are huge piles of masonry, many of cathedral proportions. Since most of these buildings are used only one hour per week, the wear and tear on them is minimal, which means that replacement costs are negligible.

Plant owned by the churches other than buildings for worship include hundreds of hospitals, homes for the orphan and the aged, colleges, universities, military academies, secondary schools, mission stations, etc.

Nor must we forget the real estate holdings such as office buildings, farms, hotels, bars, slum housing (highly profitable), and assorted other businesses, including companies which manufacture goods all the way from religious publications to padded bras. The Church comes by these seemingly unrelated enterprises by inheritance,[9] or by a deal which has manifest tax advantages for the company and the Church.[10]

[9] The author knows of one church-related institution which acquired a piece of real estate that housed, among other things, a thriving bordello. It was decided that, though immensely profitable, the operation of this type of business on what amounted to church property was a potential public relations problem and the bordello's lease was not renewed. Administratively,

PERSONNEL

The present Christian Corporation picture looks a lot better to us when we reflect on the army of dedicated ecclesiastical executives stockpiled in the countless boards and agencies of the denominations, not to mention such firmly established religious bureaucracies as the National Council of Churches, state councils of churches, and city councils of churches. The average layman is unaware of this great tangible asset to the Christian Corporation because these executives are seldom visible. This is because, when not hived away in their offices writing memos to other church executives, they are in the air, constantly crisscrossing the continent and indeed the world to attend meetings and conventions where they carry on high-level conversations with other church executives.[11]

CUSTOMERS

Even if business has fallen off a little lately, particularly on Sunday morning, the Christian Corporation still counts over 60 per cent of the population as customers. At least, over 60 per cent of the population claim they are customers. They boast some kind of allegiance to the Christian establishment. The application of

---

some difficulty arose over which executive would visit the madam and tell her she was out of business, as this was regarded as a desirable assignment.
[10] For those ignorant of tax law, a church which owns a girdle factory (there is at least one such case we know of) doesn't pay any income tax on the profits therefrom. This, as you can see, gives the religious establishment a distinct advantage over the business corporation. The IRS has been getting a little testy over this lately, but a judicious investment in skilled lobbyists ought to preserve our claim to special treatment.
[11] Just as the sun never sets on the British Empire, or didn't until recently, it is the proud boast of the Christian establishment that at any moment, around the clock, dozens of bishops, board secretaries, and lesser ecclesiatical personnel are in the air en route to some vital and crucial church meeting.

modern sales and promotional techniques to the exploitation of this market could more than double the business we are now doing.

Another positive thought we should embrace to ward off the encroachment of melancholy is that the Christian Corporation is doing something most beneficial for people. We must never forget that religion is good for people. At least, it is good for good people, as eminent theologian Rheinhold Neibuhr has told us— and it is mostly the good people who make up the Church nowadays.

THE CHURCH—A CLUB FOR GOOD PEOPLE

Surely we can find no fault here. Bad people have the Mafia, Las Vegas, saloons, and the New Jersey Democratic party for their clubs. Why shouldn't the good people have the Church for their club? Good people, for example, need an institution to define sin so that they will know who the bad people are and avoid them, and be able to feel morally superior to them.[12]

Religion is also good for people because it provides them with harmless and even occasionally useful activities. We know that many observers of the church scene complain of the millions of man hours wasted in church activities—turgid committee sessions, sleazy rummage sales, Rotarylike men's club luncheons, Woman's Society meetings whose purposes are too murky to divine, teas, sodalities, altar guilds, prayer breakfasts, etc. We would not contend that every one of these occasions is essential to anything in particular. But let us ask ourselves the question, "What would all these people be doing if there were no church activities to monopolize their time?" The answer is that they would be cluttering up the freeways, polluting our rapidly shrinking natural reserves such as beaches, forests, and rivers with beer cans, cola bottles, and half-eaten tuna fish sandwiches, and in other ways making a social nuisance of themselves.

---

[12] It is important for us to remember in this connection that sin is not the same for every Christian. What is sin for a Baptist is not necessarily sin for an Episcopalian, although there is some overlapping, naturally. Since denominations define sin in terms of things their members do not care to do, it is best if we permit each division in our New American Christian Corporation to specify what is sin for its division only.

When viewed in this light, any lingering doubts about the usefulness of church activities melt away to be replaced by deep feelings of gratitude for the good that they do.

We hope we have demonstrated through these pages, the grandeur of the Church at its best and the social usefulness of the Church even at its worst. We believe that the plan of organization for the church of the future, as we have presented it to you, fits the modern scene and answers the needs of the modern American man. With this knowledge and these insights we have imparted to you, then, you are now ready to pitch in and help build the New American Christian Corporation.

Apologia

This has been the sad story of institutionalism regnant over faith, hope and love. I have resorted to satire in the telling of it because satire, it seems to me, is more capable of carrying this kind of criticism than any other literary advice.

One unfailing retort satire elicits is, "Why do you have to be so negative?" In the case of this satire an added question will be, "Don't you find *anything* good in the history of the Church?"

Of course I find the good and the positive in the history of the Church. I find in Jesus Christ the paradigm by which to construct a truly human existence. And no one can read the story of St. Francis of Assisi and fail to be utterly charmed and lifted up. We have to remember, though, that St. Francis had his order of poor friars—which was dedicated to the alleviation of human suffering—taken away from him, put under the authority of the Church, and institutionalized. We all know what the Sadducees, the Jewish religious establishment, did to Jesus. These two examples could be multiplied by the hundreds. The bright spots were all too often blotted out by an indifferent or hostile ecclesiasticism. The seminal personalities, as a rule, were stifled by a hierarchy which saw in them a threat to its security.

If the community of faith has a future—and I think it has—its hope lies not in the ecclesiastical institution, no matter how cleverly redesigned and updated. The hope lies in these seminal personalities who have the power to renew it.

The best example of such a personality in our time was Pope John XXIII. John saw clearly what so many churchmen both Roman and Protestant see only dimly if at all—that the winds of change in the world are no longer gentle zephyrs but are whipping up to gale proportions, and the Church had better cope with the storm lest it be blown away.

But it was not as a reformer that the world honored him. When he died there was a great and sincere sense of loss felt by those without the Roman fold as well as those within it. Protestants, Jews, and those who are identified with no organized religion at all expressed deep regret at his passing.

How does one account for this? Was it a superb job of press-agentry which had built up the public image of the pope? I think not. The public, gullible as it may be at times, is capable of spotting a phony when he is as much in the public eye as was John XXIII. It was mourning the death of a good man, an extraordinary human being. Somehow John had become the symbol of the best in human personality. There was an earthy quality about him that said to us, "Here is a man who loves life, who enjoys every day, who appreciates God's good creation, who is subject to the same temptations which plague us, who, if his generous figure was any sign, came eating and drinking as did his master Christ, and who, like his master, enjoyed nothing so much as good fellowship with his friends."

He was a man who, from the start of his ministry, was very much involved with life in the real world. He made the most of his opportunities to serve. Because he was so close to the pulse beat of humanity he understood better than so many of his more isolated ecclesiastical brethren the needs, the hopes and fears of mankind. He was, in short, the kind of person all of us would like to be but aren't. He was a good, gracious, humble human being and a Christian first, and an ecclesiastical dignitary second. People sensed this and responded to it.

What John XXIII understood so well was that a church is for serving the needs of people, and therefore has no business manipulating people so that they will conform to the needs of the institution. Churches—Roman, Protestant or whatever—do not learn this lesson easily.

The late Bishop James Pike was also one of these seminal personalities in which, I believe, the Church has its hopes for the future. More abrasive than Pope John, a man of a constantly inquiring mind and restless, questing spirit, he was—like John—impatient with a religious institution which refused to examine its time-hardened creeds and fusty procedures lest it lose some measure of its power and privilege.

Diane Kennedy Pike, the bishop's widow, writes in her recently published book *Search* that in the 1960s the bishop "plunge(d) into a re-examination of not only his own theological premises, but those of the Church. He sought not so much to bolster the tenets of faith as they had been passed on for generations as to look anew at the way things are and then evaluate the Church's verbal formulations of truth in the light of reality as a twentieth-century man knows it."

This is the kind of activity in which the Church should always be engaged. Whether one agreed with Jim Pike or not, it is to the religious institution's discredit that, though a bishop of the Church, he finally had to leave it.

Only a few years ago the religious controversy was theological in nature. Today the focus has shifted to reform and renewal of the religious institution. There are emerging styles of Christian community quite unlike the standard parish church. There is constant experimentation in the forms of public worship. The impact of the religions of the East is making itself felt, especially upon the young, and Christianity may be moving in the direction of an eclectic faith.

Those who have read this book should know, though, that any reformation or renewal is likely to relapse into a new institution which sees people primarily as customers, as consumers of the institution's product. This is why we stress that the real hope is to be found in the Pope Johns and the Bishop Pikes who will not hold still for this sort of thing.

There is a paucity of such personalities, at the moment, within the religious institution, but there are some, and there will be more. Cardinal Cushing, commenting on the death of Pope John, said,

"I do not expect to see his like again." Perhaps not. But God in His wisdom and mercy seems to raise up men for the Church's hour of need. Luther was such a man. Wesley was such a man. John XXIII was such a man. It is unlikely that the ingenuity of the Almighty is yet exhausted in this regard—and that is the best hope of all.

CHARLES MERRILL SMITH
KEY BISCAYNE, FLORIDA

March 12, 1970